T0311518

Cambridge Elements

Elements in Critical Heritage Studies
edited by
Kristian Kristiansen
University of Gothenburg
Michael Rowlands
UCL

HERE AND NOW AT HISTORIC SITES

Pupils and Guides Experiencing Heritage

David Ludvigsson
Linköping University

Martin Stolare
Karlstad University

Cecilia Trenter
Malmö University

Shaftesbury Road, Cambridge CB2 8EA, United Kingdom

One Liberty Plaza, 20th Floor, New York, NY 10006, USA

477 Williamstown Road, Port Melbourne, VIC 3207, Australia

314–321, 3rd Floor, Plot 3, Splendor Forum, Jasola District Centre, New Delhi – 110025, India

103 Penang Road, #05–06/07, Visioncrest Commercial, Singapore 238467

Cambridge University Press is part of Cambridge University Press & Assessment, a department of the University of Cambridge.

We share the University's mission to contribute to society through the pursuit of education, learning and research at the highest international levels of excellence.

www.cambridge.org
Information on this title: www.cambridge.org/9781009517195

DOI: 10.1017/9781009327374

First published 2024

A catalogue record for this publication is available from the British Library.

ISBN 978-1-009-51719-5 Hardback
ISBN 978-1-009-32738-1 Paperback
ISSN 2632-7074 (online)
ISSN 2632-7066 (print)

Here and Now at Historic Sites

Pupils and Guides Experiencing Heritage

Elements in Critical Heritage Studies

DOI: 10.1017/9781009327374
First published online: May 2024

David Ludvigsson
Linköping University

Martin Stolare
Karlstad University

Cecilia Trenter
Malmö University

Author for correspondence: Cecilia Trenter, cecilia.trenter@mau.se

Abstract: The study explores the meaning-making of cultural heritage in school field trips to five sites in the region Östergötland in Sweden. It treats the materiality of the place and experiences of the guides and the pupils, obtained in school as well as in other contexts, as meaning-making resources during the site visits. It emphasises that sites should be seen as processes, open to interpretations and reinterpretations. The visitor is steered by expectations and common values as well as by the ways in which the heritage site is displayed and presented. In the present study, both adults (guides) and children (pupils) are defined as visitors. The authors draw on theories from history education research and from heritage studies when interpreting how pupils encounter heritage sites; they underline the centrality of 'the flesh and embodied agency' in the experience of sites. This title is also available as Open Access on Cambridge Core.

Keywords: field trips, elementary school, performativity, materiality, heritage sites

ISBNs: 9781009517195 (HB), 9781009327381 (PB), 9781009327374 (OC)
ISSNs: 2632-7074 (online), 2632-7066 (print)

Contents

1 Introduction

Temporalities, Materiality and Performativity

In this Element, we approach critical heritage studies by investigating field trips at the intersection of school contexts and cultural heritage practices. Our contribution to the existing field is to explore heritage sites not only as complementary teaching aids, but as important resources for learning. So far, explorations of historical empathy and affections in relation to encounters with the past have largely been made in connection to classroom settings to measure in which ways or to what extent the pupils have learned history (Bartelds et al., 2020; Endacott & Brooks, 2013; Endacott, 2010). In this approach, much of the focus is directed at the teacher's choices, actions and interpretations of the content highlighted in their teaching. However, and importantly, in accompanying school groups to historic sites and studying the interaction between pupils and the past, we have noticed that teachers rarely have a prominent role. What takes place at historic sites is more often an interaction between the pupils, the site and the guide; that is, a person who tends to approach cultural heritage from other perspectives than that of the school curriculum. Certainly, guides are very influential interpreters of cultural heritage (Macdonald, 2006; Quinn & Ryan, 2016). However, some studies on guided tours have suggested that guides and tourists should be seen as 'co-producers' of the guided tour (Larsen & Widtfeldt Meged, 2013). Inspired by such research, and based on the cases discussed in this study, we question the idea that guides should be seen as the leaders (who define the heritage site) and the pupils as followers (who learn history at the site). Instead, we propose that the pupils are important agents in their own right, with a significant ability to influence their own experiences and learning at the sites.

We take our starting point in the theoretical fields of the material, affective, performative and haptic aspects of the field trips and theories in history education. The emphasis on embodied experience such as emotions and haptics put materiality and performativity in the centre when studying experiences of the past. How do the physical conditions of historic sites – objects and artefacts, weather, accessibility – affect the visitors' experience of the past? The historic moment that the guided tour presents at the site creates the opportunity for temporal explorations through experiences, feelings and knowledge about the past in interaction with other people and with the materiality of the place. It is in this encounter between people, historic moments in history and physical and material resources that the (meaning) making of the space takes place.

2 Theory and Method

Theoretical Standpoints

Bridging Theoretical Fields of Heritage Studies and History Education

An important field of research has sought to address the educational aspects of museums, heritage and historic sites (Lonergan & Andreson, 1988; Ludvigsson, 2012), emphasising the potential to encounter the past that heritage may have for young people. These and other studies have demonstrated the complex links between the sensory and cognitive systems (Martin et al., 2000; Tiballi, 2015) and the importance of historical empathy for developing historical understanding, and thereby the relevance of affection and emotions in learning processes (Bartelds et al., 2020; Barton & Levstik, 2004; Endacott & Brooks, 2013; Kohlmeier, 2006). In addition, other researchers have investigated sensitive topics or traumatic histories in relation to heritage (De Nardi, 2020; Marcus et al., 2012; Spalding, 2012; Trofanenko, 2014) and the making processes of heritage through embodied experiences (Lovell & Bull, 2018; Smith et al., 2018; Tolly-Kelly et al., 2018), including representational and non-representational studies in which the performative agency of visitors is in focus (Smith, 2021; De Nardi, 2020).

Three focal theoretical points steer our research on the dialectic between visitors and heritage sites. *Firstly*, due to the potential variety in interpretations and meaning-making, heritage sites are contentious. We want to emphasise that sites should be seen as processes, open to interpretations and reinterpretations, and that the importance of heritage sites cannot be easily separated from the individual or group that experiences the place (Crouch, 2016; Harrison, 2013; Smith, 2006; Smith, 2021). *Secondly*, historic sites can be interpreted in different ways, but not in just any way; the visitor is steered by expectations and common values as well as by the ways in which the heritage site is displayed and presented. In the present study, both adults (guides) and children (pupils) are defined as visitors, although they occupy apparently different subject positions, with an agency of display – the guide from a guide perspective and the pupils from the everyday context in school. We draw on theories from history education research and from heritage studies to identify tools for interpreting how pupils encounter heritage sites. *Thirdly*, in line with this performative approach to space and sites, critical heritage scholars have underlined the centrality of 'the flesh and embodied agency' in the experience of sites (De Nardi, 2020, p. 13). Recent research argues that our engagements with heritage are figured through the politics of affective registers such as pain, loss, joy, nostalgia, pleasure, belonging or anger. The idea of affective practices is based on

Margaret Wetherell's emphasis on the sensual experiences, and on the affections and emotions that are born from it. Affective practices point towards a non-dualistic position in learning processes, where the sensual and bodily material dimensions are intertwined with the discursive cognitive aspects (Wetherell, 2012). Aligning with De Nardi, who studies visualisation of places by drawing on affective theories by Wetherell et al., we argue that places are never abstract because 'social knowledge [is] always situated somewhere' (De Nardi, 2020, p. 20). A point of departure in this Element is the 'haptic approach'; that is, the notion that humans are connected to the surrounding physical environment. The bodily sensations and responses that naturally occur as part of experiences. In this sense, one can speak of haptic knowledge, which involves relationships between the visual, the non-visual and the somatic senses (Lee, 2005; Massey, 2005; Paterson, 2009). Haptic knowledge can be related to 'knowledge by acquaintance' and the role that sensory experiences can play in a knowledge process (Ludvigsson et al., 2021; Trenter et al., 2021; Winch, 2013).

Meaning-making Experiences in History Education Research

The starting point for the study is, as emphasised above, that places and cultural heritage are performative and created. The meaning-making experiences of visitors, both pupils and guides, have the epistemological residence in phenomenology's 'lifeworld'; that is, the perceived and subjective world in which individuals live their lives.

We argue that there are action offers (affordances) of places and cultural heritage (see, e.g., Achiam et al., 2014; Gibson, 1979). It is by no means given what a particular place represents, as different interpretations are always possible. Pupils, as a group but also individually, can perceive different affordances offered by the place, which is why different places can be created simultaneously at the same site. In this study, we lack empirical material to shed light on this process at the individual level; instead, we discuss the construction of sites on the group level. The role of materiality when experiencing the past can be related to Zerubavel's (2003) discussion of how historic sites and objects can serve to establish a link with the past. This is well in line with arguments made in history education research. Through visits to historic sites, and in encountering cultural heritage, pupils are thus given the opportunity to engage with the past in different ways than are usually possible in a classroom. The differences between the numerous forms of experiencing the past can be described using the concepts *erfahrung* and *erlebnis* (Arthos, 2000; Carr, 2014; Gadamer, 2004; Tapper, 1925). In the classroom, learning is articulate, cognitive and reflective (*erfahrung*). Relations to the past are indirect, mediated and moderated by the teacher and the resources used, such as textbooks. The visit to a historic site and the encounter with cultural heritage includes *erfahrung*, but can at the same time represent something less steered; namely, an offer of meaning that is less filtered than in the classroom, more direct, unreflective, subjective and bodily (*erlebnis*), which occurs in the encounter with the materiality of the place. Our study emphasises the interplay between different ways of experiencing the past, between *erlebnis* and *erfahrung*, in the negotiation of places.

In our collected material, three groups of actors are represented: guides, pupils and teachers. We have chosen not to focus on the teachers' perceptions of the meaning potential of the places. One reason for this is that the teachers' role during the visits to the historic sites is less prominent than that of the guides and the pupils. Another reason is that we have discussed teachers' perceptions and use of visits to historic sites elsewhere, from a didactic perspective and within the framework of teaching history (Stolare et al., 2021).

Stock of Knowledge, Knowledge by Acquaintance and the Importance of Imagination

In the next few sections, we explore the meaning-making of cultural heritage in school field trips to five sites, underpinned by the idea of performative agency. We thus treat the materiality of the place and experiences of the guides and the pupils, obtained in school as well as in other contexts, as meaning-making resources during the site visits. These experiences, or the 'stock of knowledge' to quote Selby (2016), gain importance in the meaning-making of the historic site, both during the site visit and the interviews by the pupils conversing with each other and with the guide and the interviewer. Selby explains the visitors' encounter both with the site and with other visitors in terms of performance. During the visit, different layers of knowledge are activated and collectively negotiated between visitors to the site in order to make sense of both the visit and the site. The 'stock of knowledge' primarily revolves around everyday experiences and shared knowledge about the past. For pupils, knowledge of the past can be based on what has been learned in school before the excursion and may be practised during the visit. Not all classes included in the study had received instruction in the historical period relevant to the tour; however, the pupils generally had some prior knowledge. This knowledge may, but need not, consist of a common historical canon. References to famous figures or events appear in our material both in the guides' stories about the places and in the pupils' questions and comments. These common references to the historical canon serve as an important part of the negotiations on the value of the site. However, and importantly, we believe that cultural heritage and historical canon are not necessarily the same thing. The historical canon can consist of fragmented clusters of names and years, such as 'Gustav Vasa was the first king of Sweden', or insights into historical inaccuracies such as 'The Vikings did not have horns on their helmets' or 'Marie Antoinette never said the phrase "Let them eat cake"'. The historical canon may consist of knowledge obtained in school about overall processes, such as industrialisation or the emergence of the modern welfare state. Cultural heritage, on the other hand, may coincide with the historical canon, but has been estimated to be worthy of preservation for the future through cultural heritage policy. By cultural heritage, we mean the staging of the site that confirms its historical value in a local, national or international context. Cultural heritage does not have to consist of a historic site, but can include, for instance, collections in museums. Not all historic sites are cultural heritage. This study is based on site visits to historic sites that are defined as cultural heritage. This is not to say that the participating school groups visited these sites because of their value as cultural heritage. Rather, these sites were chosen because they are located in the school's immediate environment and can be linked to the school syllabus.

Knowledge by acquaintance connects existing knowledge, including canonic historical knowledge of the past, to the situated experiences from heritage sites. Included in the wide definition of knowledge of the past that shapes the experiences at the site is the common knowledge of field trips as canonical cultural experiences, shared by generations of people who have visited particular places in their region. Within the framework of this study, the sites also serve as representative places in the sense that they offer concretisations of the period of history from ancient times up to the 1800s which pupils study in the first six years of Swedish compulsory school, encompassing the history of the nation and the early history of the kingdom. One of the sites included in this study, the Alvastra monastery ruin, is also an established part of the traditional itinerary for the region of Östergötland, which generations of pupils have carried out, often in year 4, and covers ancient and medieval cultural heritage sites in the western part of the county.

No interviews were conducted with pupils or guides before the excursions, nor were their experiences or preconceptions mapped in any other way. However, some parts of the guides' and pupils' previous experiences are obvious and spelled out; the fact that the field trip is conducted under the auspices of the school and that the group consists of pupils indicates that any preparations for the visit undertaken at school are present in the negotiations and meaning-making.

Knowledge can also stem from universal human needs. The pupils may be able to perceive that their own needs are much the same as those of people who lived in the past. For instance, people in the past used to cook, but they did it in a different way than we do today. They would have needed to get up to go to the toilet at night just like we do, but they used pots rather than toilets. This fact created an idea that seems to lead to an experience more direct, unreflective, subjective and bodily, it carries the nuances of *erlebnis*. In the awareness of those parts of existence that can be related to universal needs, it becomes possible to let go of one's own present for a brief moment. Transforming practical experiences and needs into insights into the history of a place requires imagination, where the already experienced is translated into a new (historical) context (De Nardi, 2020). Imagination can thus be used to create an insight into the historic site, becoming a tool for communicating and negotiating with others – between visitors and between guide and visitor – about the site (Trenter et al., 2021).

Temporalities and Performative Experiences of the Past

Aspects of historical change such as causes and consequences, and alternative interpretations of historical processes, are difficult to mediate during guided tours, which tend to favour a polarisation between 'now and then' – between visitors and the past presented at the site. In the course of the study, we will challenge the idea that guided tours build on a fixed point in time, a 'frozen moment in the past'. Rather, as our cases will illustrate, heritage sites are often linked to several historical stages and periods at the same time; for example, a castle or palace that has been inhabited for several hundred years and whose interiors span several eras. It is common that the display of a place is based on a given context, such as the late 1800s at Löfstad Palace; medieval monastic life through the Cistercians who lived at Alvastra; or the construction of the Göta Canal at Motala mill site. Yet, while the point in time that is highlighted during the tour can be specific and concrete – that is, a particular date and place – it can also be a vaguer narrative abbreviation (Rüsen, 2005) that refers to an era or process where the concretisation of the history through an object, a point in the landscape, a story or other condensation of the narrative is presented in the display and guided tour (Erll, 2011).

The complexity of place, space and time has been explored by researchers who problematise how the present at a heritage site triggers a simultaneous understanding of temporality. Mikhail Bakhtin's concept of the chronotope describes how narration, time and space are created in fiction through densification and embodiment of time by the artist (Bakhtin, 1981). The term 'chronotope' has been used as a theoretical tool to describe how historic sites are created by artistic and aesthetic means (Axelsson, 2003; Gustafsson, 2002). Other scholars have investigated how visitors perceive places defined as cultural heritage sites, frequently entangling participants' experiences and thus creating an emotionally saturated atmosphere that is unpredictable and blurs the boundaries between time and space (De Nardi, 2020; Sumartojo & Pink, 2018). We argue that the consequences of performativity in relation to experiences of time suggest that the only fixed points in time are the very moments during the visit and interview; that is, a performed 'here and now'. The complexity of temporalities in which the past and present are blurred when performed at the site and in the interviews means that heuristic tools are needed to interpret the meaning-making of the sites in terms of learning about the past. Based on history education research, we study how the interaction between pupils, place and guides mobilises proximity and distance in time (contemporary as well as past) in a way that problematises the division between now and then by creating multitemporality.

Methodological Considerations

Method

The cultural heritage sites covered in the following sections are all located in the province of Östergötland, in southeastern Sweden. This region has a varied landscape with cultivated plains, large forests, cities and coastal areas. There are a number of traces of the past, such as natural traces of the Ice Age; petroglyphs and runestones from the Viking Age; churches, monasteries and castles from the Middle Ages; noble palaces, battlefields and agricultural areas from the early modern period; industrial areas from the 1800s and 1900s; as well as a number of historic buildings from different periods that are preserved and cared for by local heritage associations or by state or regional authorities. Over the past 200 years, the region has experienced emigration, urbanisation and, more recently, immigration. This historical, mainly agricultural county has undergone significant change, and today most of the inhabitants live in the two large cities of Linköping and Norrköping. A common feature of the region's historical traces is that to a large extent, they represent key parts of Swedish national history. Linköping was a key location for the emerging royal power during the Middle Ages, Norrköping was the country's first and long-dominant industrial town – Sweden's version of the English city of Manchester – and Vadstena Castle was one of the strongholds of the royal Vasa dynasty.

The study's focus is on the guides' and pupils' descriptions of what happened during the excursion, what they perceived as important, and how the different senses came into play during the site visit. One or two researchers accompanied each field trip, making audio recordings and taking field notes. The researchers attempted to stay in the background, being present but not intruding during the activities. Sites were documented photographically. The interviews followed a semi-structured form. With the guides, individual interviews (about thirty minutes long) were conducted, which were designed to include more general questions about tours and the location, since the guides' experience of tours was based on many more tours than the one observed for the study. The recent excursion was used as a concrete example. The pupils were interviewed in groups of four or five. The pupil interviews, which were about fifteen minutes long, focused exclusively on the experience of the excursion just undertaken, but also included associations and reasoning from, for example, lessons in school and experiences from the pupils' lifeworlds. Thus, the experiences of the place are examined in different ways in the pupil and guide interviews. The guides are not presented as individuals but rather are interviewed as representing a certain position, namely that of professional guide or representative of the site. The pupils are allowed to interact with each other as individuals during the field trips and interviews but are steered by the peer culture in the class, and by the fact that the field trip took place in school.

The relationship between guide and pupils is at the centre of the analysis, as well as their relationships to the historical period/cultural heritage value that is tied to the place. Since the pupils were interviewed in groups, and the pupils interacted with each other during the visit, the negotiation between the pupils about the value of the place as cultural heritage becomes relevant in the study (Kvale & Brinkman, 2009).

By choosing visits to cultural heritage sites that bear both similarities and differences, we have aimed to by inductive methods explore the similarities and differences between sites, relate to the character of the place as cultural heritage, the relationship to the past that the guide and teachers promote and the pupils' activities during the visit.

Within the framework of the project, about ten school classes were observed while visiting heritage sites, and a relatively large number of interviews were conducted with pupils, guides and teachers. The sites were selected to represent different parts of the cultural-historical landscape, and included historic agricultural areas, monasteries and churches, historic house museums in palaces and workers' homes and historic industrial areas (Ludvigsson et al., 2020).

The data collection was carried out in 2017, 2018 and 2019. One of the authors (Ludvigsson) photographed the sites; collected information documents provided by the sites; documented the class visits with audio recordings and field notes; photographed drawings and stories that pupils produced in the classroom after the visit; and interviewed guides, teachers and pupils (Drew et al., 2008). It is conceivable that during the observation and/or subsequent interviews, guides, teachers and/or pupils were influenced by the presence of the researcher, although there are no clear indications that any of them adapted their behaviour to the interviewer. Guides, teachers and pupils were informed in advance that participation in the research project was voluntary, and that the aim of the project was not to evaluate, nor would it affect the pupils' grades. Some of the guided tours clearly followed a script that would have been the same whether a researcher had been present or not. Nonetheless, it is entirely possible that the researcher's presence may have led participants to adjust their behaviour or comments. Some guides may have wanted to make a good impression and therefore prepared more thoroughly than otherwise would have been the case or tried to give the appearance of being well prepared. The researcher's status as a historian may have caused him to be perceived as an authority on the historical period at hand and may have led to the participants seeking confirmation rather than talking freely about the past.

The study involves primary school pupils and their classes, with the majority being between ten and twelve years old in upper primary (years four to six). However, in one case (Bomtorpet), the pupils are in lower primary (year three) and are nine years old. It is worth noting that history becomes a separate subject for pupils in Swedish compulsory school starting from year four in upper primary. In lower primary (years one to three), history is integrated with other social studies subjects such as civics, geography and religious education. Extensive efforts were made to inform pupils and their guardians about the study and to obtain informed consent. In some cases, however, pupils were not able to participate because their guardians did not submit a consent form (Balen et al., 2006). For ethical reasons, all participants have been de-identified. The study has been approved by ethical review in Sweden.

The collected material has undergone a qualitative content analysis. The interviews and site visits were documented via audio recordings and field notes, which were then transcribed in full. In order to capture the performative actions that took place during the interviews and fieldtrips, all sounds – such as laughter, sighs, cries and similar non-articulated verbal expressions and noises – were transcribed. Knudsen and Stage make a historiographic distinction between researchers for whom affect is beyond language categorisation, which force the focus to signs of affects, and those who regard language as being capable of expressing affects, in other words that there is no contradiction between the categories of language and the categories taking part in the social shaping of bodies (Knudsen & Stage, 2015, p. 4). Our study approaches this epistemological dilemma by considering connections between categories of language on the one hand, and sensorics and haptic bodily categories on the other. To be able to include a wide range of the data we use analytical strategies presented by Knudsen and Stage, namely characteristic communication of affects, such as outbursts, broken language, hyperbole, redundancy; non-verbal communication, such as laughter and bodily gestures; and also communicative content about experienced or attributed affect, as when people describe how they feel (disgust, fear, amazement) mediated during the excursions or in interviews (Knudsen & Stage, 2015, p. 9; Ludvigsson et al., 2021; Trenter et al., 2021). The participants' bodily expressions are evaluated together with their verbal expressions to investigate their reactions to the sites. Knudsen and Stage also acknowledge certain challenges in collecting and producing data. How can the researcher define and measure affects and bodily experiences? This study uses different types of data collection, namely first-hand data-mediated 'in situ' – that is, in the situation when the affect is happening; or mediated as remembrance – that is, when the person who has experienced the affect communicates the experience in retrospect.

Knudsen and Stage further distinguish between 'emic' perspective (produced by the one who is in the affect) and 'etic' ditto (observed by someone else) (Knudsen & Stage, 2015, p. 8). The present study focuses on etic aspects; that is, observations by people mediating affections both 'in situ' and remembered. The 'in situ' is performed by participating in the excursion. However, we consider the interviews as equally 'in situ' for historical experiences; when participants remember collectively, or individually, and recall the excursion by talking about it, affections are both remembered and re-experienced, and are sometimes subject to new affections. Since we consider the experience of the site as an ongoing process, we define the interviews, although they were conducted some days or up to a week after the field trip, as also being experiences of the historic site.

Regarding quotes from the empirical material, it should be noted that all dialogues conducted during observations and interviews were in Swedish. For this publication, quotes have been translated into English. Inevitably, some linguistic nuances may be altered in translation; however, we have attempted to focus on the essence of the points made in dialogues between pupils, and between pupils and guide.

The Five Historic Sites and Cultural Heritage

The choice of historic sites was informed by their accessibility for schools and pupils. All of the selected places are used to receiving pupils on excursions. The five sites selected for this study represent different aspects of historic Östergötland. We use the term 'historic site' as a description of the actual material places, all of which consist of settings where history has taken place; they have all been regarded in their own time and retrospectively as important sites in a national or international perspective, either by virtue of the uniqueness of the place (e.g., a castle where a peace agreement was signed or a factory where a decisive strike started) or as representative of a certain type of phenomenon (a medieval church or a sawmill from the era of industrialisation).

Two of the chosen historic sites – the cathedral in Linköping and the ruin of the Alvastra monastery – were built during the Middle Ages when Östergötland was a core area in the Swedish kingdom and part of Catholic Europe. Both places are included in the Swedish national historical canon due to their respective positions in medieval political history. Linköping Cathedral was built in the Middle Ages and is one of the largest church buildings in Scandinavia. The construction of the cathedral went on for centuries. It has since been rebuilt and altered many times, yet is considered to have largely preserved many medieval features. Nicolaus Hermanni, a bishop and key political actor during the 1300s, worked in Linköping Cathedral, and he was also close to Saint Birgitta and her daughter Katarina. The cathedral is still used today as a place of worship. It is located in the centre of Linköping and occupies a clearly visible position in the urban space, near the city's squares and the train station. The guided tour that features in this project was a time travel role play for ten- to twelve-year olds. The role play is based on a script developed by church staff. In addition to the building itself, the materiality of the building includes props consisting of replica clothing, herbs, wax tablets and incense, as well as the fixtures of the church interior. The location is well defined for the purpose of the visit. The time travel element is indicated by the ringing of a bell, upon which the visitors are taken back to the year 1381, during the Middle Ages. The historic site becomes a place by virtue of its historical authenticity as a church, along with the props and staff who lead the role play, creating a clearly defined chronotope.

Alvastra, Scandinavia's first Cistercian monastery, was founded in the 1100s by King Sverker's queen, Ulvhild. The monastery was run for 400 years, before it was closed in connection with the Reformation in the 1500s. Today, Alvastra is a ruin. Parts of the monastery's limestone walls have been used throughout history in the construction of other buildings in the area. As part of Swedish national history, Alvastra is a famous and popular excursion destination, located on the eastern shore of Lake Vättern, some forty miles from Linköping (Axelsson, 2003). The ruin is also a regular stop on a traditional itinerary around western Östergötland. The tour that the project participated in was given to a class of ten-year olds and led by a freelance guide with Alvastra as one of her specialities. The materiality of the site consists of ruins and traces of the rooms in the monastery and abbey church, as well as certain plants found in the surroundings which were used by the monks. The guide uses pictures of similar monastery gardens in the tour. Since it is a ruin, the place requires the staging of notions of what the site would once have looked like.

Löfstad Palace is one of many palaces in the region that were built in the early modern period, and represents a time when the nobility had great power and vast wealth, in Sweden as in other European countries. The palace is weakly connected to the Swedish historical canon due to the fact that the sister of Axel von Fersen, the lover of French queen Marie Antoinette, lived at Löfstad; however, the historical value of the palace lies in the building representing the lifestyle of Swedish nobility for the past 300 years. Löfstad was originally built in the 1600s in Sweden's so-called Great Power Era. The palace was given its current design in connection with an extensive renovation during the 1700s. The palace is a typical historic house museum. Emilie Piper, who was the last owner to live there, transferred the palace to Östergötland Museum for preservation in 1926. Inside, the palace is fully furnished, and looks much as it did the day Emilie died. However, it also contains objects belonging to those who lived there in the centuries before her. Therefore, Löfstad Palace gives a good insight into the kinds of homes that were inhabited by the nobility, the very highest circles in Sweden (cf. Meurling, 2008; Sylvan, 2010). The palace is located near the E4 motorway, 170 km south of Stockholm. The tour for eleven- to twelve-year olds included in this project was led by a staff guide during a standard tour of the palace interior, including the 'ghost room' number 13, which is not usually included in the standard guided tour. The materiality consists of inventories and artefacts organised in a contemporary staging that corresponds to Emilie Piper's organisation of the home from the 1920s, and includes wallpaper, furniture, utensils, clothes and textiles.

Löfstad Palace is staged according to a narrative that reflects Emilie Piper's life, but also her own ambitions to stage earlier eras in the palace's history. The materiality both guides the narrative of the historic site and forms the basis of the guide's story about the palace. Löfstad Palace is a well-defined chronotope in the sense Bakhtin defines the phenomenon: by aesthetic means and staging, the milieus at Löfstad appear as frozen moments in time – one being the exact moment that Emilie Piper died, as her bedroom remains exactly as it was on that day. Other rooms in the palace capture moments from earlier periods, resulting from Emilie Piper's lifework 100 years ago.

The soldier's cottage Bomtorpet was originally inhabited by a soldier and his family. In Sweden (and Finland), the soldier's cottage was a simple croft built for and used by the local soldier in the permanent keep (military tenure) from the beginning of the 1680s. Each village financed a soldier by providing the cottage, which remained even after 1901 when national service took over. Soldier's cottages are today frequently present in toponyms and materialised as buildings in urban environments as well as in more desolate areas. Despite its military origins, the soldier's cottage is part of a past civil society whose history can be traced, since military source material contains the names of soldiers who have lived in the croft. Bomtorpet can therefore be seen as a historic house museum. The soldier names in the form of given names – for instance, adjectives such as 'Kind', 'Witty' or 'Strong' – were assigned to the soldier when he enlisted and can still be found in contemporary Swedish surnames. The soldier's name was usually associated with the soldier's croft, and would also be given to his successor. The croft Bomtorpet ('Bom' is thought to be a reference to the 'boom' noise of a gun) dates back to the 1700s. Today, it is surrounded by modern buildings. Here, the countryside has been transformed into a suburb that can be reached by city buses. The croft with outhouse and root cellar is managed by the local heritage association, two members of which led the guided tour for a group of nine-year olds. Bomtorpet is filled with objects, collections of artefacts from different contexts and eras that are linked to the cottage and to Sturefors, the village named after the Sturefors estate. The historic site is a well-defined place by virtue of the cottage's position in the local community and the type of cultural heritage, the soldier's cottage, and is a defined chronotope through its value as heritage.

The Motala mill site, finally, is located right next to the Göta Canal, a huge artificial waterway which here represents industrialisation, modernisation and the great transformation of the old society in the 1800s, and can be considered an important part of the Swedish historical canon. The Motala mill site can be characterised as an open-air museum. The industrial area from the first half of the 1800s is preserved. Old industrial buildings are scattered throughout the area, each with its own specific features. There is also workers' housing. The adjacent Göta Canal is still used for boat traffic. The focus on the workers' labour and everyday life is reminiscent of Bomtorpet's depictions of ordinary people's living conditions, but the exposure of materiality sets them apart. The tour included in this project was led by an employed guide who escorted a class of ten-year olds around the workers' housing. While the Motala mill site stages specific years in the workers' housing, the material environments in Bomtorpet consist of collections of artefacts from different eras that have the place as a common denominator. The Motala mill site is a tangible site and materially well-defined cultural heritage site and chronotope by virtue both of its collections and of its position by the canal, which was historically important for industry and fishing.

These five case studies form the empirical part of the study presented in Sections 3 and 4. Section 3 deals with the Alvastra monastery ruin and a tour for pupils in year 4; a tour of Motala mill site also for year 4; and a role-playing activity at Linköping Cathedral with year 5 pupils reliving 'the Middle Ages in the Cathedral'. The choice of these three cases is justified by the fact that all of them include planned participation of the pupils during the visit. At Alvastra and at the cathedral, pupils' participation involves different forms of bodily and sensuous experiences through active participation during the visit. Both sites are characterised by being less object-dominated – consisting in Alvastra's case of ruins and walls, and in the cathedral's case a place of worship. The time period treated during these two visits goes back more than 500 years into the past. The Motala mill site consists of environments characterised by physical traces of the relatively modern history to be conveyed. The participation here consists of the visitors' (teacher and pupils) dialogue and interaction with the guide during the tour.

Section 4 deals with two cases, Löfstad Palace (year 5 pupils) and Bomtorpet (year 3). These two displays can be considered more traditional museums in that they contain rich collections of objects and clear physical traces of the history to be conveyed. In addition, these tours were guide-oriented. The relevant historical period in each case dates back between 100 and 400 years. The interaction between guide and visitor group in both cases takes place in the form of the guide's commentary to the pupils in combination with the pupils' questions to the guide. One difference between the two cases is that Löfstad Palace does not represent part of the pupils' everyday experience, while Bomtorpet is a more integral part of their local community and daily life.

3 Alvastra, Motala Mill Site and Middle Ages in the Cathedral

Alvastra

Alvastra: The Visit

The guide meets the pupils, a Year 4 class from the nearby school, at Kungsgården, located adjacent to the Alvastra monastery ruin. After the visit to the ruin, the class walks a few hundred metres to visit a modern farm. The theme of the day is food production; this theme will also characterise the guided tour of the monastery. Prior to the visit, the pupils have not studied the medieval period, but it is due to be covered in class soon.

The pupils are led by the guide between the different rooms of the monastery – or rather what remains of them. Since this is a ruin, as can be seen in Figure 1, only the walls and parts of the floors of the buildings are preserved; it is the

Figure 1 Alvastra monastery ruin. Photo: Niels Bosboom, 2006. CC-BY-SA 3.0.

Source: Wikipedia.

guide's task to reconstruct the place by narrating and describing it. While the guide does this, the pupils ask spontaneous questions. In this way, they shape the place together. However, it is the guide who ultimately sets the tone. The teacher is in the background, making occasional comments and handing out apples to the pupils.

The visit to the site is physical: the pupils walk on the stone slabs that make up the floors and feel them under their feet, while touching the limestone walls. In their experience of the site, the ruin, the narrative given by the guide and their own imaginations are all essential elements that make up a total possible experience. The guide creates situations where pupils, with their bodies and minds, get the opportunity to discover the site firsthand. This strategy becomes evident at the beginning of the visit, where pupils are allowed to climb through a narrow aisle to get to what was once the monastery's dining hall.

> P1: That tunnel we went through, did it use to be a tunnel?
> G: Now I didn't hear what you said at the beginning there.
> P1: The tunnel.
> G: The tunnel. It was a stove, so we have just climbed through the stove, you might say. Because the heated room was next to it. Then we have the

kitchen to that side and now we are standing in the dining hall. Hmm. So, they were self-sufficient. Yes?

P2: Did they have grass on the floor [as there is now]?

G: No, they didn't. Usually there were paved floors.

(Observation Alvastra)

By walking between the walls, and visiting the different rooms and buildings, the pupils get an idea of how the monastery was laid out. The pupils come from a nearby school and have previous knowledge of the site; several have been there before. However, in their interactions with the guide, their historical frame of reference appears limited.

The focus of the visit is the monastery itself and the lives of those who lived there. The guide describes how cold it could be during winter, since only one room in the monastery was heated. The pupils' interest is aroused when the guide reveals that the monks used to carry around small dogs to keep warm when it was cold. When the guide then revealed that the monks consumed four litres of strong beer daily and therefore probably walked around slightly intoxicated, the guide got a spontaneous counter-question from one of the pupils: Were there children in the monastery and what did they drink? The guide answered that there were few children in the monastery and that they too were given beer, but that the beer was then diluted with water. Pupils gasped, and some giggled when they heard the guide's response. In the guide's story, an emphasis is generally placed on how different the lives of the monks were, compared to their own.

In the narrative that emerges during the visit, the guide tried to establish a pedagogic comparison between then and now. When the group is standing in one of the monastery's gardens, the guide asks the pupils if they know someone who grows vegetables in pallet frames, to which several pupils quickly reply that they do. The guide goes on to describe that this was something that the monks also did; they used boxes that were specially designed to facilitate weeding. In this sense, the site's cultivation system becomes a link between then and now.

The guide tells the group that the monks harvested pears and cherries. The class visits the place where the fruit trees are supposed to have grown, and the guide shows photos from other contemporary (preserved) monastery gardens. When they enter the abbey, the guide stops and points to a plant. What is that? she asks them. Rhubarb, some pupils answer. Butterbur, the guide replies. It is a species that the monks introduced into the area. The guide picks a plant and breaks off the stem. She passes the plant around, urging each child to smell the liquid that seeps out of the stem:

P1: It smells nice!

G: Pass it around, then we'll see.

G: Do some of you think it smells like something else?

P2: I just think it smells good.

P3: Citrus.

P4: Soap.

G: Has everyone been able to smell it?

G: I heard, some of you actually thought it smelled like soap. I'll pick up on that. It was in fact, that in this [plant] there's a substance, and if you were to rub this leaf in water it would get frothy. And that substance is called saponil. Sapo in French actually means soap. So we think this one was used for cleaning products. It may also have some antiseptic effect. To be used for washing away bacteria and cleaning wounds and such. And in the 1300s, in the 1300s there was a terrible disease called the plague that came here.

P4: Yes, I said that.

(Observation Alvastra)

Here, the plant becomes something tangible linking the pupils to the time of the monks, through its use as a kind of soap, something that the pupils use every day. Moreover, they can now hold in their hands the same plant that the monks used 700 years ago.

A challenge with Alvastra monastery as a learning environment is that it is a ruin. In the absence of objects, the site itself and the plants that grow there must connect the pupils to the past. After the forty-minute guided tour, pupils are invited to explore the monastery on their own, and are clearly instructed that they are not allowed to climb the ruin walls. After a while, the guide reassembles the class. She then carefully instructs them to stand in a particular place, in a passage between two rooms in the ruin. Once they have gathered there, she tells them that extensive excavations of the ruin have been made. She asks them if they know what an archaeologist does, which they reply they do. The guide then reveals that right where they are standing, under their feet, the remains of monks have been found buried in seven layers. The ground beneath the pupils' feet thus links them to the monks and the Middle Ages.

Alvastra: The Guide's Voice

Uses of the Past and the Guide's Perceived Mission

In the interview, the guide states that her wish is for the pupils to have 'an aha experience, "this has actually happened where I live"', and to learn about how power was centralised to the monastery and the surrounding area. She describes the place as a backdrop for the history to be learned, which is experienced on site and therefore offers more than, for example, an image displayed in the class-room. The experience of the site can include sights, smells, sounds and tactile experiences, and the guide's commentary becomes secondary in relation to the physical experience of the place. 'I think it is a lot to take in, but at the same time, it can help reinforce what you are saying. If they remember ten per cent of what you say, it might be good enough . . . that ten per cent has been boosted by all that other stuff.'

The guide emphasises how history changes along with research. 'It was not like that when I was a kid; it was fixed, but in this place history has been rewritten several times.' The guide then gives examples of developments in archaeological research on the ruins of Sverkersgården and Sverkerskapellet, located near Alvastra.

Materiality of the Site

Since the cultural heritage site is a ruin, the tour takes place outdoors, and the guide explains that she therefore needs to take the weather into account; the wind, for example, can make communication difficult. The level of preparation of the groups when it comes to appropriate clothing also affects the guided walks. Pupils from the countryside tend to be dressed as the site requires, while children from the town can arrive in sandals, according to her experience.

The guide uses maps during the walk to concretise the site. Pupils are given a map with tasks to complete, such as counting windows in the ruin. The pupils' imaginations are also exploited to bridge the lack of physical traces and the distance in time to the Middle Ages. The guide mentions the example of the monks warming themselves with dogs to stage the story.

Although the site is a ruin, the guide believes that the pupils can perceive the monastery as a grand building with walls, as a place that they can enter. According to the guide, the children experience the visit as an adventure which triggers historical thinking. Further, their imaginations are mobilised with stories based on myth and legend: 'Nothing is known for certain about the monastery treasure, but it is still part of the site,' explains the guide.

The Pupils and the Site

The guide states that she adapts the tour to the primary school curriculum. 'I get the impression that the year 4 pupils I meet have learned about their region. It is because of that that they do the traditional school trip around the region. While year 5 pupils have come [while studying] both the Viking Age and the Middle Ages. Then the visit is more about monastic life.' She emphasises that it makes a difference that the pupils generally come from Östergötland, the region where Alvastra is located, and therefore the site is a familiar place and part of their previous experience. The guide expresses a sense of fellowship with the pupils and other visitors through the site's status as part of the regional cultural canon:

> This [Alvastra and the Rök stone] is a classic class trip and I meet people who say, "I haven't been here since I was on a school trip". Then it doesn't matter if it's an 80-year-old, a 50-year-old or a 20-year-old standing there, they have this reference. Then I think it has left its mark, obviously. It's made them remember it, obviously. Then again, you may not remember which century and such, but the place has definitely left an imprint.

The pupils are integrated into the tour through treasure hunts, tasks to be solved or dialogues with the guide about objects and stories. The guide uses these strategies to strengthen the connection between the site, the pupils and the perceived history. The children are tasked with solving a riddle in pairs, yet they are encouraged to do it without talking, thus illustrating the vow of silence under which the monks and nuns lived. The guide has a clear plan for adapting the tour to the specific grade and syllabus. It is as if the guide has a flexible 'now' from which to start the tour, adapting to the group's starting point and supposed prior knowledge. She has a well-thought-out approach to how the site can be displayed to compensate for the shortcomings of the ruin; that is, its lack of artefacts and written primary sources.

The guided tours are instrumentalised through educational arrangements in the form of tasks and challenges that the pupils complete together (fellowship around the activity), an imposed 'vow of silence' (connection to the monks' living conditions), and gamification as a method, through treasure hunts and riddles to be solved.

The negotiation between pupils and guide about the meaning of place and a recognition of the pupils' 'erlebnis' are calculated and integrated into the guided walk; the children's play becomes a medium for conveying the past. There is also the connection to the site that is conveyed in other ways than through the educational structure of the tour. The guide's relationship to the past encompasses a multifaceted view. She is aware that the past is negotiated, for example, in research about the site, and that our view of the site will continue to change in line with new research findings. The guide's relationship to time is not multifaceted but rather unified and interconnected; she recognises a common reference point in the traditions of the regional school trip that creates a community that bridges time and space between generations, who have all attended materialised historic sites that are part of the collective memory of Östergötland as a place for school trips.

Alvastra: The Pupils' Voices

Uses of Heritage at a Well-Known Site

All of the pupils interviewed state that they had been to the Alvastra monastery ruin before, and some had been there 'many times'. They had visited with their families for a barbecue, to play hide-and-seek or to take a family photo; someone's younger brother had participated in the local chronicle game (a kind of history play) that took place next to the ruin, and one pupil points out that the site is a popular venue for wedding ceremonies and wedding photos. The pupils also mention having been there to pet the animals at the farm next door. They characterise the ruin as beautiful, saying it is 'fresh and natural', possibly hinting at its qualities for being clean and well-preserved. Clearly, the monastery ruin constitutes a familiar setting for the pupils. They also refer to relatives who have told them about the monastery and the monks. However, none of them had been on a guided tour of the site before.

The fact that the pupils now had access to a guide characterised the visit in several ways. One pupil emphasised that now when they explored the ruin, they could ask the guide what the different rooms were. Thus, the pupils perceived the guide as an essential source of knowledge for the information she offered and the opportunity for question-and-answers that her presence entailed. The pupils said it was easy to follow the guide, and that she spoke in a way that they could understand. To some extent, their confidence in the guide can be explained by the fact that they knew her as the mother of a pupil at their school. Thus, both the guide and the ruin were already part of their lifeworlds.

No references were made in the interviews to what the pupils had previously learned in school. However, this is not surprising, since the class had not yet studied the Middle Ages or dealt with any of the kings who had a connection to the monastery. In fact, this particular visit to the ruin was carried out because an opportunity suddenly appeared to have the expenses for the bus trip covered, if the visit to the ruin was combined with a visit to the farm next door. The lack of preparations may be one reason for the vagueness with which the pupils spoke about the period of history when monks lived in the monastery. Even the guide in her presentation chose to speak about the time of the monks as a period rather than a specific year. The lack of preparations may also explain the fact that during the interviews, several pupils referred to the monastery's 'lay brothers' mentioned by the guide as being children, as the Swedish word for 'lay brothers' (lekbröder) is similar to the word for 'play' (leka). However, lay brothers were in fact the men and boys who were responsible for manual labour and secular affairs in the monastery.

Materiality of the Site

When the pupils were interviewed in groups, a couple of days after the visit to Alvastra, materiality and imagined materiality came to the fore. They stated that the guided tour had given them a better understanding of the place, and made it easier to imagine the long-demolished walls and ceilings that existed when the monastery was up and running. The pupils were helped to understand specific details of the ruin, such as the 'cool' holes that might have been sinks:

> P1: I thought these holes were cool because you didn't know what they were. It looked like a toilet though it was something completely different kind of.
>
> P2: I also liked that sink thing.
>
> P3: What I like about Alvastra is that if you find something, you might think it is something, but it may turn out it's something completely different.

Thus, the material traces of the past play a role in arousing the pupils' interest, even in cases where their meaning is uncertain. A more imagined materiality can be found in the pupils' references to King Gustav Vasa (who has been called the founder of modern Sweden), who had stones collected from the monastery for the building of his castle in nearby Vadstena. They attribute their knowledge of Gustav Vasa to the fact that a person at school had dressed up as the king and given a presentation about him. A connection to the king that several pupils apparently found intriguing was the legend that the monks hid the treasures of the monastery before the king came and confiscated them. The treasure has never been found, they say, and speculate that it might be found before they become adults, unless it is a myth. This is a rare example of how pupils articulate a future dimension in conversations about cultural heritage sites. One pupil says she saw a stone in the nearby Vadstena Castle that was marked as having come from Alvastra.

Experiences of Heritage Embossed by the Pupils' Lifeworlds

During the interviews, pupils often reacted to each other's comments. These small exchanges show that the cultural heritage experience is characterised by the pupils' social relationships and experiences from their lifeworlds. When the pupils ponder the difficulty of knowing what it was really like to live as a monk in the monastery, one of them points out that there are still nuns today, and that he has met a nun on one occasion. When they recount the guide's statement that the monks, and even children in the monastery, drank beer daily, they note that this is not how things work today. Something else they think a lot about is who did the work in the monastery, since during the visit, they got the idea that children in the Middle Ages had to work:

P1: They had dogs and they had lay brothers.

P2: I think it was a bit strange that there were lay brothers cause it was only the monks who lived there.

P3: I thought that the guide said: they had lay brothers, they were the only ones allowed to play. [This interpretation is a result of the similarities between the Swedish words for 'lay brother' and 'play']

P2: They worked. It is a bit strange that it was mostly the children who got to work, and the women get to cook and work in the kitchen and do laundry and things like that . . .

P3: I don't want to live like that . . .

P2: I guess the men helped quite a lot as well, but it felt like the children worked the most, kind of. And nowadays, the parents work the most because we have to go to school and learn things.

The dialogue is characterised by the notion that the 'lay brothers' in the monastery were children and that it was they who mainly had to do the work. The dialogue illustrates the pupils' explicit comparison between now and then. 'Today', the parents do most of the work, while during the time of the monastery, it was the children who worked the most. The pupils perceive this as 'strange', a clear indication that they perceive the past to be a foreign country, and the comment 'I don't want to live like that' can be interpreted as if the pupil identifies himself as a potential 'lay brother', and does not like the idea of such a life.

The pupils' lifeworlds are intertwined with their musings about life in the monastery as they try to imagine the life of the monks. During the visit to the ruin, the pupils learned that the monks had dogs, and this information proved very important for how they imagine the monks' sleep:

P1: I still think it must have been quite noisy [in the monastery when the monks went to sleep] because they didn't have so many animals, but I think the dogs . . .

P2: . . . barked a bit . . .

P1: . . . yes they barked a bit and maybe there were many birds and many animals that disturbed them kind of because it was a beautiful monastery.

P3: When I'm asleep and my dog sees me, he tries to jump up into my bed . . . he jumps up to my face and licks me in the eye.

P4: We had a dog . . . she was good at jumping and then she jumped up into my bed and laid down on my back, she was not that heavy, and then she barked in her sleep. . . .

P2: . . . then my cat came in and started meowing, then she jumped up in the bed and lay on my lap, then I woke up when she jumped up, because then she took her claws and went like this.

P1: I wonder if they [the monks] had cats?

P2: I don't think they did. Nuns did. Nuns had cats and monks had dogs.

Thus, the pupils associated from the historical dogs to their own pets. Their own experience with pets lead them to imagine that the monks lived with their animals in a similar way. This is a clear example of how the pupils' lifeworlds influence their understanding of the past. It almost seems like the pupils are trying to trump each other with stories about how they have had their night's sleep disturbed by pets, while at the same time, it also seems realistic to them that the monks slept with their dogs. The pupils also visited a farm in connection with the visit to the monastery ruin, and several of their comments indicated a great interest in animals; for example, that they really wanted to extend the visit to the farm because they hoped to see a heifer that would calve.

Overall, the pupils' conversations about the visit to the Alvastra monastery ruin were characterised by elements of the guide's story, by their own experiences of the physical site and by an imagined materiality. Further, it is striking that the pupils made so many references to their own lifeworlds in the form of previous visits to Alvastra and Vadstena, to their previous experiences and thoughts related to animals, and their opinions on how children should live. Their fantasies about life in the monastery are based on their own experiences that relate to the guide's stories.

Motala Mill Site

Motala Mill Site: The Visit

The class of Year 4 pupils and the teacher arrive by bike at the open-air museum Old Motala Mill Site (Gamla Motala Verkstäder). It is June and very hot. Today, they are going to learn more about the canal builder Baltzar von Platen and the mechanical industry that emerged along the Göta Canal during the 1800s. The pupils will get to immerse themselves in 'their' local history. They are well prepared: several lessons have been devoted to von Platen and the construction of the Göta Canal. They will use this knowledge and experience during the day.

A guide meets the pupils and takes them around the various exhibits housed in the old industrial area. The guide establishes clear and direct contact with the pupils early on. It turns out that she has met the pupils before in a different context, which seems to make the interaction easier. The interplay between guide and teacher is developed throughout the tour. The teacher does not hesitate to interrupt and ask the pupils questions about what they are experiencing. The guide takes a position reminiscent of a teacher: she shows and educates the pupils about the place. She often uses the initiate–response–evaluate (IRE) model of questioning, and the pupils do not hesitate to ask questions. The guide is constructing the tour; however, the pupils play a very active part. Together, the pupils, the guide and the teacher construct the place. The guide explicitly links to the frame of reference that the pupils have gained through their education at school. The site, buildings and objects displayed in the various exhibitions inspire the pupils to ask spontaneous questions about what they see and experience.

An essential dimension of the visit is that the pupils have the opportunity to wander between the historic buildings; sometimes, they walk around only for a minute, and sometimes they take a longer walk. The area with remaining factory buildings can be seen in Figure 2. The walking seems to have a function: by walking the site, the pupils get to experience the organisation of the place physically, through their bodies. Thus, they are given the opportunity to experience how the buildings, with their different functions, are located in relation to each other along the Motala river. In this way, the historic site is constructed, and this is done in interaction with the historical frame of reference that the pupils have built through their schooling.

The interplay between the lifeworld of the past residents and the pupils' frame of reference established during lessons in school developed through the visit. In the beginning of the visit, it was essentially the historical frame of

Figure 2 Motala mill site is located by the Motala river and the Göta Canal. In the nineteenth century, the smoke from the mills coloured both workers and buildings black; the black colour is largely missing at the site today. Photo: Carl Schnell, 2022. Published with permission from Motala kommun.

reference that was addressed. Gradually, however, there was an increasingly clear connection made to the pupils' own lifeworlds and experiences. The key connection was made by comparing their own living conditions with what was shown in the exhibitions. One exhibition described the harsh life conditions of the workers who dug the Göta Canal in the early 1800s, reconstructing the workers' sleeping quarters with beds and life-size mannequins lying in them. The pupils reacted to how close together the workers lived and how narrow their beds were. Some pupils tried to tickle the mannequins lying in the beds, which the teacher prevented them from doing. Thus, the desire to interact with the exhibitions and objects was strong; the pupils wanted to touch and feel.

> P1: Don't touch.
> G: This is how the workers slept, the ones who worked digging the canal.
> P2: Is someone laying up there?
> P3: Did they sleep in pairs?
> G: Yes, two by two. It was very crowded. Surely quite disgusting as well. So very crowded, but then they worked so very hard during the day that once they got to rest, they would sleep like a log.
> [–]
> P4: Let's see here.
> G: You shouldn't touch there. They can be quite fragile. I think you shouldn't touch. Leave them alone.
> P5: [grunts]
> G: No don't touch, don't touch. Look but don't touch.
> P5: I'm boxing him, then he'll wake up.
> G: I said that [responding to another pupil].
> P6: I want to tickle him [the mannequin lying in the bed].
>
> (Observation Motala mill site)

The exhibits are not treated as closed stories by the pupils, and objects play a vital role in this. It is mainly through their lifeworlds and physical experience that the pupils are able to connect to the narrative presented in the exhibitions.

The connection to experience and to the pupils' lifeworlds becomes particularly clear when, towards the end of the visit, the class is allowed to enter a house where two working-class homes are displayed, one from the mid-1800s and the other from the turn of the century, c. 1900. As can be seen in Figures 3 and 4, these homes are tiny and cramped – but that does not stop the pupils from exploring the rooms and pointing out different artefacts that interest them. The guide describes the living conditions of the families who would have lived in the homes and thus puts the rooms in a historical context.

Figure 3 Museum apartment in Motala, furnished as in 1853, with an open fireplace. Photo: Carl Schnell, 2022. Published with permission from Motala kommun.

With the teacher's support, the guide tries to draw the pupils' attention to the changes that society underwent in the second half of the nineteenth century and which are illustrated by the homes. The guide's stories of the two homes differ. When talking about the older of the homes, she emphasises how different it is compared to what homes today look like. However, when talking about the home from the early 1900s, the starting point used by the guide is rather to point out the similarities with the pupils' own homes, rather than the differences. Here, the tendency is that past and present merge; the room from the turn of the century almost represents the present. The pupils recognise many of the objects that are displayed and express their own relationships to them.

The artefacts in the homes take centre stage. Special attention is paid to the furniture, clothing and items relating to cooking; that is, objects that relate to basic needs, and which the pupils also have in their own homes, although they may look somewhat different. By connecting the rooms to specific historical actors, the homes come alive; they appear authentic. The authenticity is also something that arouses the pupils' interest. When visiting the home from 1902, pupils began to ask questions about what they saw. Where did the artefacts actually come from? The power of the exhibition is based on the idea of

Figure 4 Museum apartment in Motala, with furnishings in accordance with a probate from 1902, with the wood-burning iron stove in the middle. A potty can be glimpsed on the floor to the right. Photo: Carl Schnell, 2022. Published with permission from Motala kommun.

authenticity, that the different objects on display really were once used by people living there. In the guide's narrative, these were real homes. However, the pupils challenge this narrative as they begin to apply a meta-perspective on what they are experiencing.

> P1: I have a question. Did they use these things for real? Or are they just kind of similar?
> G: Exactly, these are similar artefacts.
> Teacher: These things have been used, but in other places?
> G: Exactly, exactly. They've collected together old things that are supposed to show how people lived here. They have been used but in other places than here. Just as you say.
> P2: Is there something that was used in this actual room that is still here?
> G: I'd think the stove perhaps. It could be. But that's probably all.
>
> (Observation Motala mill site)

The objects are significant since they seem to open up the narrative. As the objects connect to the lifeworld of the past residents, they link this lifeworld to the historical frame of reference that pupils have acquired in the classroom. In this way, there is the potential for the pupils' historical understanding to be deepened by what they experience through the exhibition.

Motala: The Guide's Voice

Uses of the Past and the Guide's Perceived Mission

The guide interprets her task as 'telling [visitors] about local history and showing them the industrial area and the value of the place. Show how it was, covering the facts'. Since the guide has a positive experience of cooperating with teachers, she presents the connection to previous teaching as natural:

> I think it's great that the teachers are active [in the visit]. I am impressed with the educators, the classes are well informed and engaged. They connect [the visit] to what they have read before, like saying "Do you remember, we read this" while dealing with noisy children. There will be nice connections between here and their classrooms. It should be a given resource in learning about Motala's history. My unit is under the education division, so it feels reasonable to work with schools.

Materiality of the Site

The site is a museum containing objects, but the museum is also built around environments, both the factory buildings and workers' living quarters. Pupils are allowed to touch the items at the museum, but the guide says it can be difficult to pass objects around in larger groups so therefore she avoids doing that. References to smells serve as a way to concretise what it was like in the past. The chamber pot in one of the working-class homes is the object that arouses the most glee. However, even objects unknown to the pupils play a part during the guided walk, as the guide describes their function and also reveals something about what life was like at that point in history.

The guide describes having occasionally conducted tours in the form of time travel, 'such as pretending that the pupils are a newly hired group of workers I am showing around the site, and it works pretty well. I change clothes during the walk and then [as a consequence] is moved forward fifty years. But you miss a lot then too, [it's] hard to say what perspective one should apply.' Since the museum depicts societal changes over time, the guide does not want to be tied down to a certain period in history, as in the time travel exercise, since this makes it difficult for her to refer to wider processes of historical change. The guide points out that when she conducts tours in period outfits, the clothes mark who the guide is and who is in charge of education in this setting.

The Pupils and the Site

The guide did not have direct contact with the teacher before the visit, although she had 'happened to hear that they had worked on [canal builder Baltzar] von Platen, but most people in Motala have. They brought a lot of knowledge and got to demonstrate it.' She stresses that she considers it vital that when the pupils get 'a little noisy', they not only play around but that they start thinking about what they are experiencing. The guide says that she always has the frame for the story prepared, but that the pupils' questions can change the order in which different aspects are addressed during the guided walk. When asked whether input from the pupils has ever led to a different focus of the guided tour, she replies that their comments can sometimes give her insights: 'After one guided walk, someone asked where did they shower, and then I thought I have missed out telling them that there were no showers.'

The guide tells of another guided tour where the original plan was overturned when a mouse ran across the floor. The guide says she jumped out of her skin, but the group of visitors, who had dementia diagnoses, were unfazed by the incident.

According to the guide, the pupils' background does not play a significant role in the guided tour, except when pupils have Swedish as their second language:

> Then a lot of [the conversation] is based on the life conditions in their respective home countries. "We had one of those lamps in Syria and we were this many people living together" ... I read the other week that many new arrivals [to Sweden] live in overcrowded homes and then you must be careful not to ... I want to show that we are better off today, but [sometimes] it does not fit, because people are still poor today.

The guide strives to deepen the factual knowledge about history by stimulating the pupils' imagination and empathy to show what life was like during the period at hand. Thus, she stimulates the pupils' 'erlebnis'. The guide's multifaceted relation to various time periods means that it becomes problematic for her to step into any one historical role, as by doing so she locks herself into a particular moment in time. Entering such a role makes it impossible to tell the story of a different period that the historical figure, bound in her time, cannot possibly know about. However, historical clothing is still used by the guide as it can serve a purpose in the sense that it is as a marker of who is pedagogically responsible for the tour and, on a more general level, contribute to pupils feeling that they are visiting another time.

As indicated by the example treated just above, contemporary injustices can make it difficult to use certain aspects of the present as a starting point to understand the past. Since new arrivals in Sweden today may experience vastly different living conditions compared to those who are already well established in the country, it is no longer possible to assume a certain standard of living among pupils and compare this to how the Motala workers lived.

Motala: The Pupils' Voices

Visiting a Cultural Heritage Site as an Integrated Part of Education

In the group interviews, the pupils were very enthusiastic about visiting the Motala mill site, which was part of a longer bicycle excursion, where they also visited the graves of canal builder Baltzar von Platen and his horse. The pupils reflected a bit about these graves and how it was that no one had scribbled on von Platen's gravestone. They also wondered what the horse's skeleton looked like.

When the pupils talked about the Göta Canal and its construction, they referred to what they had learned in school, but also to knowledge that they gained through the visit: 'We learned [during the visit], but we had talked about it before.' One of the pupils referred to British canal builder Thomas Telford and stated that he had seen a video about him on YouTube, while others referred to things they had learned from their teacher. Thus, the pupils were well aware that Motala's history was closely linked to the canal, the local factories and Baltzar von Platen who, according to the pupils, was rich, powerful and 'cunning'.

Materiality of the Site

Many pupils commented on the historically reconstructed workers' housing they had visited with the guide. They accurately referred to the fact that the exhibits represented the homes of working-class families in 1853 and 1902. This knowledge probably stemmed from the fact that on returning to school, the class and their teacher had discussed the excursion and, among other things, written up key dates on the board; whiteboard notes can be seen in Figure 5.

The pupils referred to several objects and interior details in the workers' homes. However, they were particularly interested in the fireplace in the apartment from 1853, which they had been told could get very smoky, and sparks could fly out 'so a fire might start'. The pupils recalled that the guide had said these problems only occurred before the home had an iron stove (which was installed from 1902), and one pupil considered that the guide was 'in love' with the iron stove and its oven. Clearly, the guide had made them think about the importance of the fireplace and the iron stove, since they mentioned the smoke, the risk of fire and how these things affected the possibilities for cooking. The pupils made positive comments about the guide. They especially appreciated that she had been dressed in historical clothes, which made her 'fit

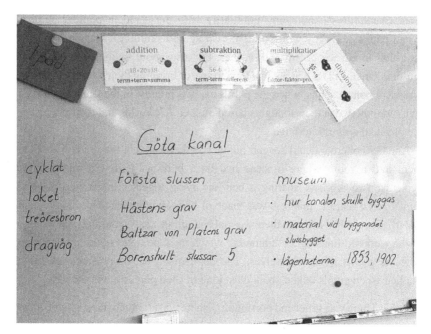

Figure 5 A summary of the class's excursion to the Göta Canal and the Motala mill site was written up on the whiteboard in the classroom. The summary mentions the horse's grave and the apartments from 1853 and 1902. Photo: David Ludvigsson, 2018.

in' with the past. However, it puzzled them that they had also met her at another museum the class had visited – and one of the pupils claimed that he had run into her in several different supermarkets; she was simply everywhere.

Another object the pupils were fascinated by was the chamber pot under the bed in one of the workers' homes. They carefully accounted for the fact that the people who had lived there went to a privy or into the forest when they needed to defecate, but used the pot if they woke up at night when it was cold and dark outside. The pot became the subject of lively dialogue and thus constituted an example of 'heritaging' in the pupils' internal dialogue. The pot sparked several pupils' fantasies about faecal matters, and one jokingly pointed out that you could not go out into the woods and pull down your underpants because then an animal might come and eat your private parts.

Experiences of Heritage Embossed by the Pupils' Lifeworlds

The mill site and surroundings near the Göta Canal were familiar to several pupils, who said they had cycled to the canal with their families to watch boats and eat ice cream and waffles. They asked the interviewer if he had seen the

Göta Canal films[1], indicating familiarity with the canal in popular culture. When pupils said they would like to visit again in future, it was partly about returning to eat ice cream and waffles, but also about visiting the industrial museum that the class had not had time to see, or bringing their parents to see the historical homes. Thus, when the pupils express interest in the site, one can see an overlap between their thoughts based on their lifeworlds and their interest in the physical cultural heritage.

Another concrete detail several pupils recalled was that the guide had taken them into a room where a scene had been built with life-size mannequins depicting two workers sharing a bed and lying together under one blanket. Pupils noted that the mattress was made of hay. They understood that the men had to share the bed because there was not enough space. Accordingly, they spoke of the workers' housing as 'cramped', which must be understood in relation to how the pupils lived themselves. The comparison to the present was made implicit when pupils talked about what kind of food people ate in the past.

> P1: There was gruel and porridge. . . . there wasn't much meat, maybe there was meat but there wasn't much anyway. But they ate a lot of fish because it could be found in the stream right next door.
>
> P2: A lot of raw fruit or whatever it was, root vegetables. Potatoes and stuff.
>
> P3: Food was very scarce in the 1800s. And then when we came to the 1900s . . .
>
> P1: . . . yellow carrots . . .
>
> P3: . . . when it comes to the 20th century, then there was a lot of meat around, so then people would eat, and potatoes. . . .
>
> P4: It was very poor kind of in those days. . . .
>
> P1: The yellow carrots . . . parsnips . . .
>
> P3: You just put it into the oven . . .

The pupils talk over each other about gruel and porridge, about meat being scarce, about the fish in the stream, and about parsnips ('yellow carrots') which seem unknown to them. The dialogue probably helps them to remember various things, and several pupils are involved in referring to different vegetables. All in all, the conversation shows an understanding that the people who lived in these houses were poor and did not have much food. The relative lack of food is emphasised in an implicit comparison with the present when there is plenty of food available in supermarkets, which pupils know well from their everyday lives.

---

[1] 'Göta Canal or Who Pulled the Plug?' (1981–2009) is a Swedish comedy film series, directed by Hans Iveberg.

Middle Ages in the Cathedral

Middle Ages in the Cathedral: The Visit

A class of Year 5 pupils, together with their teacher, waits outside Linköping Cathedral. Next week, they will start studying the Middle Ages, but today they are going to have their first encounter with the period. After a while, a man in medieval clothes (a bishop's vesture) appears. 'Salve!' he says. This means 'Welcome'. 'I think I know who that is,' one pupil exclaims spontaneously. 'It's the wife!' 'No, that's not quite right,' the man replies. A woman, also in medieval clothes, interrupts. 'Who are you, then?' she asks. 'I am a bishop. My name is Nicolaus Hermanni,' the man replies.

This is how the time travel exercise begins, where the medieval cathedral in Linköping is used to give pupils an experience of what it was like to live in the Middle Ages – more precisely, in 1381. Time travel is simulated in the form of a role-playing game. The frame story is that the construction of the cathedral has dragged on. The situation has become grave, as there is a lack of construction workers, which is why the bishop is now asking the pupils to help. Behind this idea is a team of staff at Linköping Cathedral, who have been staging the time travel activity for several years. Different members of the team take on the leading roles in the role play, namely the king, bishop, housewife, abbess, building contractor and school master.

Before the pupils are allowed to enter the church, which appears in Figure 6, they are divided into three groups: some become novices (nuns), while others become schoolboys or stonemasons. The researcher accompanies the schoolboys group. The pupils change into medieval clothes and are each given a name typical of the period by which they will be known during the activity. Once the clothes are on, they gather for a slow ritualised countdown from now to then, from 2019 to the Middle Ages and the year 1381. Then they step into the cathedral's large incense-scented nave, where medieval choral singing sounds in the background. It is with the help of the medieval building with its scents, lighting and special acoustics that the time travel is constructed, to create a medieval experience for the pupils that is as authentic as possible.

The smells and sounds bring pupils into their roles and help make the transition from 2019 to 1381 believable. Despite this framing, the pupils are somewhat sceptical initially, and nervous giggles can be heard on the audio recordings. However, gradually, these fall silent, and it becomes obvious that the pupils respect the framing; they are playing along. The pupils no longer occupy the role of visitors; instead, they participate in the role play. The straightforward narrative of the time travel contributes to the site becoming time specific. In this context, the site takes on the character of a well-defined

Figure 6 Linköping Cathedral, seen from the cathedral park (domkyrkoparken). Photo: Katlinke, 2022. CC-BY-SA-4.0.

Source: Wikipedia.

chronotope (time-space). What the pupils experience is not the Middle Ages in general, but the specific chronotope of Linköping in 1381.

The pupils follow the character in the game that is linked to their group. Once inside the cathedral, the groups carry out various activities. Schoolmaster Mattias, played by a female guide, leads the pupils who are now medieval schoolboys. The character Master Mattias takes the disciples out of the building in order to show them their living quarters. To get outside, they need to open the large cathedral gate, something the pupils are asked to do while in the roles of disciples. Everyone is given a task, meaning that they open the gate together.

> Master Mattias (MM): Good, can you come up here? You must help me open the gate. You may have to pull out that spring.
> P1: Yes damn.
> MM: Good. And now you step aside.
> MM: And you, you pull this lever straight down. It slams in the lock.
> MM: Good.
> MM: And you insert the key. And unlock the gate.
> P2: What a big key.

P3: Big key.

MM: So you twist in that direction. More . . . It is quite sluggish.

MM. Oops, a bit more. There. Good.

MM: Birger [the name of the schoolboy]. Lift it upwards. Straight up and open.

P4: I see light.

MM. Great, thanks for helping.

(Observation Middle Ages in the Cathedral)

They go back into the cathedral. The next step is to learn a few phrases in Latin for greetings and giving their names ('nomen meum est . . . '). In order for the pupils to be able to study by candlelight like medieval schoolboys, they each have to make a candle from beeswax tablets, which is done in a corner of the cathedral, appearing in Figure 7.

Figure 7 The pupils/disciples sat on the cathedral floor when training to write on beeswax slates. Photo: David Ludvigsson, 2018.

P1: Is this pasta?

P2: It looks like pasta.

P3: Like wafers.

MM: You can feel and smell it a little to see if you can figure out what it is.

P2: Honey, it is honey.

P3: It's a honey thing.

[–]

MM: Well, what do you think you have in your hands.

[Pupils mumbling.]

MM: Honey yes, it smells a little like honey. But honey is usually a little messier? What can it be if it smells like honey but it's not honey.

P2: Something from the beehive itself.

MM: Yes, it is beeswax.

(Observation Middle Ages in the Cathedral)

Master Mattias shows them how to make their candles. Suddenly, she starts to sing a liturgical song, 'Jubilate Deo', which the disciples learn in advance of the ceremony when the novices are to be ordained as nuns. However, before it is time for that, the disciples get the opportunity to try writing on wax tablets with long pencils made of wood, the words that they have just learned in Latin. While doing so, they can hear the other groups singing in Latin. The acoustics of the vast nave give their voices a distinctive sound.

After the pupils have been in their groups for a little more than forty-five minutes, the class reconvenes for the final episode of the time travel, when some of the pupils acting as novices are to be ordained as nuns. However, the ceremony is interrupted abruptly when the king appears and begins to accuse the bishop of not paying his taxes. The time travel ends with the pupils marching out of the cathedral in a procession with lit beeswax candles in their hands, singing in Latin the song they had learned during the hour and a half that the time travel had lasted. In the armoury, the ritual countdown is repeated, this time from then to now. Once back in the present, the pupils change back into their own clothes, and the characters in the role play hand the pupils over to the teacher.

Middle Ages in the Cathedral: The Guide's Voice

Uses of the Past and the Guide's Perceived Mission

The leader of the role play is one of the members of what she calls the 'ensemble' that performs the time travel. When asked what they want to achieve, she replies,

We want them to have an in-depth experience ... local history. Everything that has happened is for real. I have met young people [who have been here] when they were in Year 5 and studying the Middle Ages. A class from lower secondary school walked by and shouted, "They're doing the Middle Ages! ... " We want them to have the experience, remember and play ... and they think it's really exciting!

Thus, the role play leader understands it as her mission to keep a school tradition alive, which means visiting the cathedral to participate in the very popular role-playing games.

The historical narrative of the time travel and the roles that the participants are given do not consider identities in the present. For example, teachers are also given a role and, like the pupils, are transported to the Middle Ages. Contemporary gender roles are also repealed. The role play leader explains that for some years, stonemasons and disciples were played only by boys, and novices only by girls. Then a few years ago, the ensemble decided that the gender of the medieval groups would no longer be reflected in the gender of the pupils. Thus, pupils and teachers are now allocated to different groups without taking their gender into account.

Church naves that are still actively used for worship can create problems when pupils visit as part of their history education. This is something that the ensemble must take into account and avoid pupils participating in religious rituals for real, while still allowing them to experience how, for example, nuns lived in the Middle Ages. The ensemble lets the pupils playing nuns take part in vows of chastity, songs and prayers; however, during the scene where the nuns are being ordained, the 'king' and the 'bishop' storm in and interrupt so that the 'novices' never have time to repeat the vows and thus participate in a genuine religious act.

The leader of the game explains that the Christian Church was both a living religion and an important power in the European Middle Ages, arguing that it must therefore be legitimate to include Christian rituals and views in a role play set during medieval times. In other words, she distinguishes between the Church of the present and the Church as a cultural and institutional actor in the past. She points out that the past and the present sometimes clash, in their role play just as in fictional representations such as films: 'The bishop makes the sign of the cross, and so do bishops today ... However, we know that we are playing a game. If you think of a priest burying someone on film, that is not real ....'

Materiality of the Site

The materiality of physical objects in the church is not highlighted as central to the time travel. The ensemble leader refers to the magnificence of the cathedral and the big rood cross (triumphal cross) bearing the crucified figure of Jesus, which some pupils find frightening, as tangible factors that may still influence the pupils. When asked how the role play relates to the history curriculum, the educator says that she understands the role play as a complement to the lessons in school. 'You can watch a film or learn in school, but here we do it for real; we enter a medieval church.' The ensemble leader emphasises the singing, the smells of incense rising, the prayers and the candles that stimulate the senses and create the mood. In other words, imagination is central in combination with the sensuous experiences and the new identities given to the pupils – stonemasons, disciples or novices in the nunnery. The ensemble leader allocates specific characteristics and names to each and every one of them.

The Pupils and the Site

The ensemble leader says that the time travel follows a script, but that the script has changed over the years. They have adapted it to today's pupils and to new knowledge about learning processes.

> During the time that I have been here, it has changed. You can see this in old scripts [for the time travel]. There were old-fashioned words that you could not understand the meaning of. We want to make it more visual. We have simplified . . . We changed, the bishop and the king used to go around to the stations and ask for money, but children today are too unfocused . . . It is enough to have a small thing happen, and they will be distracted. Also, when the king and bishop had their dispute, the children were distracted.

The ensemble leader emphasises that while the pupils' ability to play along and get into character does not change the script, their involvement is an essential part of the time travel. For example, if a pupil playing a novice knows something about herbs, the 'abbess' will let them share their knowledge, and as an effect of that interplay, the game might even be further developed.

> Yes, it is funny when they go humming "Jubilate Deo" . . . it sticks and is quite unusual. They enjoy when it becomes a nice canon song . . . And they can feel joy from it. You can see that they find the gong exciting. I feel like we are getting at something . . . When the bishop almost gets beaten to death, and we hold candles . . . It feels special, unusual, and the teachers can let go; they do not have to lead. We tell them in advance, you can drop everything now. Some want to take the lead . . . and maybe step out of their role. If they ask about a tomb from the 1600s, I pretend I haven't heard . . . So, we're in a role; no one can ask about anything else.

Thus, the ensemble leader strives not to oscillate between now and then during the role play in order to keep it authentic. Therefore, the meanings of the place are determined (or limited) by whether the time travel is underway or not, and whether the participants are in character or not. This positioning is important, not least for the teachers who also have to adapt to the time travel and thus cannot control the pupils' experience by posing questions, for example. Nevertheless, the oscillation between past and present still occurs when the ensemble leader and the other participants move between the perceived historical space of the time travel and the present-day dimension without stepping out of their characters. The most difficult balancing act is between the place as a site of religious practice and as a historic site. In the role-playing game, as described above in this section, religious rituals are staged in a way that makes it possible to imitate them without authentically carrying them out.

Middle Ages in the Cathedral: The Pupils' Voices

Meeting Cultural Heritage in Church Premises

In the interviews, the pupils express their appreciation for the time travel exercise. Many pupils, though not all, had been to the cathedral before, but owing to the time travel exercise, they visited the Middle Ages rather than just the cathedral itself. Consequently, in the interviews, they talk about their experiences of travelling to the Middle Ages and did not comment on the building. Following their visit, they characterise the Middle Ages as strange and different, stating that there is 'a big difference between the present and the past'. Several of them say that it was fun to go into character with different names and to try out the physical tasks that people in the Middle Ages had done: 'You got to see what it was like.'

An example of how individual pupils interact with the frame narrative is that some pupils, some of whom have a foreign background, make comments that suggest that they did not feel at home in the Christian cathedral. One pupil comments that people 'had to be a Christian in those days', a statement that is part of an interview with pupils of varying ethnic backgrounds, thus quite clearly offering an implicit contrast to today's multi-religious Sweden. In a conversation about God and Jesus, one of the pupils points out that as a Muslim you are not allowed to make images of Mohammed.

Whilst in the cathedral, another pupil reacts to the scent of incense and comments on the strong smell, which can partly be interpreted as an expression that he does not feel at home in the church. Someone comments that Latin was the major language of the Middle Ages, 'like English today'. These examples show that the pupils react with different senses during the visit to the cathedral, but also that they interact with the frame narrative by building on their own unique frame of reference knowledge. The teacher assumes a background role during the time travel, concentrating on the pupils who needed special support.

Materiality of the Site

Depending on which group they were part of during the time travel, the pupils talked about stonemasons' marks, the writing practices of medieval pupils, or the symbolism of the knots on the nuns' costume:

> P1: I felt different. Especially with that nun's costume.
> P2: It was white. With kind of a black cap.
> P3: Then you had a rope on the side, with three knots.
> P2: And all three knots symbolised something. . . . Obedience, chastity and poverty, was that right?
> P4: We had to remember them. They meant different things. Kind of like you weren't allowed to get married. That was chastity.
> P3: You couldn't lie. But we did anyway.
> P4: It wasn't very good to lie.

There is a tangible concreteness in the pupils' anecdotes about how herbs like lemon balm tasted 'delicious', that it was difficult and messy to write on beeswax tablets, that it took four different hand movements to open the lock of the cathedral gate, and how it was like a puzzle to fit stones into a vault in the cathedral. These stories are primarily based on what the pupils had experienced physically, from the arranged interaction with a material cultural heritage in the old cathedral building. Clearly, some of the pupils' comments were influenced by what the ensemble members had told them. The symbolism of the knots is not immediately apparent to the uninitiated, but must have been explained to them. When the pupils who had played apprentice stonemasons say that it was difficult and 'dangerous' to cut stones and build vaults, this idea very likely comes from information told to them by the 'master builder' who led their group. The pupils also say that they learned Latin, which makes up yet another example of what they practised under guidance from the ensemble.

Experiences of Cultural Heritage and the Pupils' Lifeworlds

Other comments that the pupils made during the group interview emanate from an interplay between their impressions and experiences during the time travel and reflections linked to their own contemporary lifeworlds. The group of nuns/novices had worked with herbs, and when the pupils talk about this, in several cases they make associations with their own lives. One of the pupils explains his knowledge of herbs by saying that his family often makes pizza and uses a lot of oregano. Another pupil similarly refers to having become familiar with basil during a previous residence abroad.

The element of the time travel that caused the most reactions among the pupils was the commenced, but not completed, ordination of nuns. A boy who had been given the character of novice, and had to step forward to be ordained as a nun, characterises the ceremony as 'embarrassing'. It is likely that this reaction was related to the idea that he, as a boy, should not have played a female character. However, he explains his feelings as being due to the fact that he had to stand in front of the class 'in a weird costume'. Another pupil expresses that those who were not ordained as nuns were to be congratulated because they were thereby able to continue living a free life – a comment that implies both some knowledge of the life of nuns and a perception that a life outside the convent is desirable. Surely, this comment should also be seen as a confirmation of the values that the pupil holds in his contemporary lifeworld. When some pupils discuss that they would not want to become a nun, one points out that in the Middle Ages, a girl became a nun because her parents could not afford to marry her off.

> P1: To be a nun, you have to be a girl.
> P2: I would never want to be a nun, it seems so boring.
> P3: You had to pray seven times a day.
> P4: You kind of don't get to own anything.
> P5: You kind of weren't allowed to live your own life.
> P1: . . . I probably wouldn't want to be a nun, even if I was a girl.
> P4: Well, you became a nun because your parents couldn't afford to marry you off.

When the pupils discuss the nun's ordination and what it meant to be a nun, it seems that they negotiate the meaning among themselves, at the same time taking into account what they had learned during the time travel exercise. It is difficult to determine how much frame of reference knowledge they had learned about nuns and the Middle Ages at school, but since the visit to the cathedral came prior to their regular education on the Middle Ages, it was probably not very much. This also meant that they could hardly compare the nuns' lives with other possible lives in the Middle Ages. The comments about how nuns were not allowed to own anything and 'kind of weren't allowed to live [their] own [lives]' must therefore be understood in relation to the pupils' lifeworlds, where most of them probably have many personal possessions such as mobile phones, clothes, games and so forth. This contrast makes it understandable that it should seem 'boring' to be a nun. It is only through the final comment in the excerpt – that girls became nuns because their parents were poor – that one of the pupils explicitly tries to anchor the nuns' existence in a medieval context.

4 Löfstad Palace and Bomtorpet

Löfstad Palace

Löfstad Palace: The Visit

The guide meets the class by the palace stairs. Today, the class of Year 5 pupils is on a field trip. They will make two stops, the main one being the Air Force Museum outside Linköping. However, the first stop is Löfstad Palace, where the class will get a guided tour. Prior to the visit, the class has studied the early modern period.

The fact that Löfstad Palace is a historic site containing many authentic objects impacts what the pupils get to experience during their visit. The objects are fragile, so even before entering the palace that appears in Figure 8, the pupils are asked not to touch them; 'Look, but don't touch' is the message they receive from the guide. Thus, the pupils' opportunities to interact with the objects are limited, which also sets the framework for what the guide is able to do.

G: So, a little code of conduct before we start our tour. This is a museum. It's a private home that we are actually entering now. [–] But since it is a museum and we manage almost 35,000 objects here that we intend to preserve for the

Figure 8 Löfstad Palace (Löfstad slott) is located on a hill top. Photographer unknown. CC BY-SA 3.0.

Source: Wikipedia.

future, that is our mission, it is very important that you do not touch any artefacts because we all have salts and bacteria on our fingers that actually break down the objects. In an ordinary home it does not matter so much, because there you have to be able to use your things. But we who have reason to preserve things for the future, we are allowed to use this kind of thing [white cotton gloves]. I have that privilege today. (Observation Löfstad Palace)

What the pupils participate in is a pre-planned tour where the guide leads them from one room to another. The teacher is rarely heard on the recording made during the visit; the guide is solely responsible for the content during the tour of the palace. The pupils visit the dining room, sideboard-room, office, salons and bedrooms. The guide shows and tells. She talks about the various objects in the rooms, linking them to the people who lived in the palace. The guide's basic narrative is that of Emilie Piper and her home; however, the guide also introduces the pupils to other people who lived there, such as Sophie von Fersen, the sister of the famous aristocrat Axel von Fersen. By telling the pupils about Axel von Fersen, his love affair with the French queen Marie Antoinette and his failed attempt to save the French royal family from the guillotine, the guide connects the historic site – the palace – to a broader historical context. Her focus is on the rich inhabitants, and less so on the servants, although the latter are also part of the story (cf. Pustz, 2009).

By contrast, the pupils remain silent when the guide is telling her story. It is only while they move between the different rooms that they talk quietly to each other. Once inside a new room, they fall silent again and listen to the guide. The pupils do not ask any spontaneous questions to the guide, who in turn does not attempt to delve into any deeper interaction with them. The questions asked by the guide are of a rhetorical kind. It is the guide's narrative, illustrated by objects, that takes centre stage.

The objects and the place itself appear as teaching material that the guide provides commentary on. In the story, the guide oscillates between different layers of time. The tour pays much attention to the furniture and objects found in the rooms visited, and the guide links different rooms to different activities, times and periods. For example, Emilie Piper's bedroom belongs to the early 1900s, while the palace library and salon concern the 1700s and Sophie and Axel von Fersen. In this way, the tour is characterised by multitemporality. With the intention to link the visit to the pupils' lifeworld, the guide also makes references to the present.

The question of what really entices the pupils during their visit is an interesting one. Their interest in the historical context and the people who lived in the palace is potentially quite limited. It appears that their focus is rather on the supernatural rumours with which Löfstad Palace has been associated. It is revealed during the tour that the pupils have heard about the mysterious bloodstain found in one of the rooms, and of the ghosts that are supposed to appear there. There is also a possible connection between the palace and the pupils' lifeworld. One of the most popular Swedish YouTube channels at the time, with hundreds of thousands of followers, and run by influencers Jocke and Jonna, was on the topic of ghosts and spirit beings. The two influencers often posted videos in which they visited houses known to be haunted and tried to make contact with ghosts. The pupils in the class match the channel's target audience well, and Löfstad Palace is famous for its special ghost tours.

That it is the idea of ghosts and spirits that makes the palace attractive for the pupils becomes apparent when the guide reveals that they will get to see the bloodstain. It is the last thing they do on the tour, a bit like the intended crescendo. The pupils talk loudly among themselves as they make their way to the room, which is located on the top floor of the palace. Once in the room, the guide tells of a gun duel, of the bleeding young man who had been laid on the floor and who, in the moment of death, allegedly told those in the room that he would return from the dead. The pupils react to the stain. It is clear that it does not look like they expected. The stain is quite small and more brown than red, which does not tally with what they had imagined. Some pupils say it looks more like discolouration of the carpet, rather than blood. Clearly, the bloodstain is the highlight of the tour for the pupils, although, at the same time, it is something of an anticlimax.

> P1: I thought it would be bigger.
>
> P2: More colour.
>
> P1: I thought that it would be brown, with a bit stronger colour.
>
> P2: Yes, I knew. I've heard from other people that it doesn't look like blood, but I thought it would be a bit bigger.
>
> P3: It looks like it could be something else, it might not be just blood.
>
> P1: It might be discolouration.
>
> P3: It should have been bigger if you lie and bleed to death.
>
> P1: Yes . . .
>
> (Observation Löfstad Palace)

Finally gathered outside, at the bottom of the palace steps, the pupils and the guide thank each other for the visit and the pupils continue on to their next destination of the day – the nearby Air Force Museum.

Löfstad: The Guide's Voice

Uses of the Past and the Guide's Perceived Mission

When asked what she wants to achieve with the tour, the guide replies: 'I want the children to have an aha experience that I myself have when I see things and experience that it is exciting, and context … They can connect things, both in a smaller perspective that can be linked to something bigger.' She has a clear view of what is significant in history, telling her what the most important dimensions are:

> … to explain a social structure – because that is what interests me and made me want to study history. Because when I went to school, I thought I could do without kings and wars, it's too abstract, and I am probably not alone in thinking so. There are many visitors who come and have relatives who once worked here, and then we have to apply a worker's perspective, and I make that part of the tour. Then they get to see themselves in a context and it has meaning. It is so easy to be seduced by a beautiful environment, but you must understand where it comes from.

The guide mentions that she experiences some problems due to limited resources. She does not find the time to read historical studies to the extent that she would like, but she hopes to build a more solid knowledge base step by step.

> That is my way with history; you have to be relaxed. Some things can seem almost ridiculous in retrospect, and you must be allowed to joke about it, even if you also have to explain why it was the way it was. When I have a group of girls visiting, I address certain topics, and if I only have boys, it's more male oriented. That is one of those things that are important. If you only relate history to something big, that can make you feel small … you have to laugh and be able to poke fun at things … Just as we will one day be poked fun at … And I tell them that …

Materiality of the Site

The guide says that pupils tend to be interested in the children's portraits and in the historical, specially designed conversational furniture. According to the guide, even the pot cabinet becomes de-dramatising elements, connecting with natural functions of the human body. Because the museum is full of objects that pupils are not allowed to touch, such as fragile textiles, she compensates by varying the use of her voice as a means to vary the display rather than just 'stand and drill'. She describes that she makes use of objects in varied ways, lifting different dimensions in the narrative. When she is focusing on a female perspective, she sometimes highlights the curling iron found in the bathroom.

While it is clear that physical space has an impact on the guided walk, the guide suggests that this can be in unexpected ways: 'Sometimes when there are different groups it is necessary to start in a different room than the usual one, and then you enter the thread in a different way and then the story changes. And that's more fun for me, that the story changes.'

The guide mentions the famous bloodstain in room number 13, which, according to rumour, cannot be cleaned off. She notes that the pupils were disappointed when they saw it. 'Once they see it, it's not so cool; they think it should be red, and sometimes you have to explain why it's not. They've seen detective stories on television and have seen red bloodstains!'

The Pupils and the Site

The guide describes that she has a basic script but also tries to take the group into account, making small adjustments accordingly. For instance, she adjusts the topics she focuses on according to whether the group is male or female. The group of pupils participating in the observed tour are aged eleven to twelve, and the guide therefore makes an effort to use slightly simplified language. Tours for children take a different form:

> When we have young children, we have a different kind of guided tour, namely a treasure hunt, focusing on the excitement of the environment and the strange or unfamiliar things of the past. There are history lessons integrated into the activity. It is based on positive feeling and excitement. I mention to the pupils that there were kids working here, whom they can identify with.

The most common question pupils ask, the guide says,

> regardless of age, and even before entering, is whether it is haunted ... They ask about those YouTubers, Jocke and Jonna, who came here and wanted to do ghost shows, but as a museum we don't let that kind of production in. So I replied that they've been in the park ... They wanted to come in but we don't allow that, we have a kind of credibility as a county museum. When we have our own ghost walks, we only tell the visitors such ghost stories that exist. They're not that spectacular ... well we can tell what the staff have experienced here. But questions like that are very exciting to them ... Sometimes they ask how many people worked here ... and another [common] question is about why she [Emilie Piper] didn't get married, especially teenagers and adults wonder about that.

The guide says that she tries to be observant about what kinds of pupils make up the groups. 'If there are girls wearing veils, I address certain topics more cautiously. I'm thinking about this with pre- and post-marriage visitation rules for example ... You have to weigh your words ... It's not obvious to the girls that that's something to joke about ... They may recognise themselves in it. You have to be a little careful.'

The guide strives to convey the same view of history and feeling for the site that she has herself. To her it is vital to stress the role of ordinary people and servants in history, not least because some of the people who visit the palace have relatives who used to work there. Thus, historical time is complex and contains several dimensions of social and political history. The guide negotiates her starting point in the present in order to match the *erfahrung* and *erlebnis* of visitors; in this case, the pupils. She aims to relate to the group by listening and adapting not only to their age, but also to the presumed interests of teenagers, whether girls or boys, for example, and any cultural experiences that make the present less homogeneous and provide an obvious starting point for comparisons with the past.

Löfstad: The Pupils' Voices
Seeing Traces of the Life of the Elite

In group interviews about the visit, the pupils described the tour of Löfstad Palace as tedious; they had simply stood and listened and were not allowed to touch anything. Yet, they remembered some vivid details. Some of them talked about the fire that had burned the palace down, which the guide had mentioned, and how the maid who had caused the fire had run to the nearest lake and drowned herself.

Although the class had just been learning about the 1600s and 1700s, the pupils did not seem to find the experience of visiting a palace with authentic décor from those eras particularly interesting. However, one of them pointed out that there was a connection between the palace and a particular nobleman, Axel von Fersen, whom they had read about and whom they knew had had a relationship with the French queen Marie Antoinette, and was later dramatically beaten to death in Stockholm.

Materiality of the Site

The pupils remembered a few particular objects the guide had shown them, including a very long tobacco pipe that needed a valet to help light it, a pick up sticks game, and a toothbrush that the palace's last owner had inherited from her grandfather; to inherit a toothbrush was something the pupils found bizarre. Further, some of the pupils commented that there were a lot of paintings in the palace, which was different from their own homes, and that they felt as if they were being watched by the royal portraits in the dining room. One of the pupils thought that many of the portraits were there to show that the owner of the palace knew lots of important people. A couple of the pupils emphasised that they found it strange that the serving staff should stay behind a large screen in the dining room to avoid being seen by the dinner guests. Thus, some of the pupils' comments after the visit indicate that they considered the noble owners part of a social elite with their own norms and ambitions. These insights may have been based on the narrative given by the guide, or on knowledge that the pupils had gained during their history lessons in school, which they connected to material objects such as the screen and the paintings in the palace dining room.

Experiences of Heritage Created in Dialogue among Pupils

What the pupils talked about most was the palace's connection to ghosts. Several of them mentioned the legend that in the room where Emilie Piper had died, you could supposedly smell her perfume; this was thought to be 'awesome' and 'spooky.' Although the pupils were generally not interested in coming back to the palace (several of them had previously been there with their families), one of them specifically mentioned that she would like to come back to 'go on the ghost hunt' – a special walk held in the palace during the dark season. The pupils knew already before the visit that the palace was known for ghosts, but the detail about being able to smell the perfume of the dead Emilie Piper was something they heard from the guide. The single detail that engaged the pupils the most was the bloodstain on the floor in room number 13, appearing in Figure 9. All the pupils knew about the bloodstain prior to the visit, and they discussed it among themselves. According to the guide, the bloodstain was created after a man had fought

Figure 9 Room 13 at Löfstad Palace. On the floor is the famous bloodstain. Further, rumour has it that the wallpaper, which is peeling in places, refuses to stay on the walls. In short, the room is associated with ghosts and the supernatural. Photo: Jonas Karlsson. Published with permission from Löfstad slott/Östergötlands museum.

a duel and then bled to death in the room, but the pupils were disappointed both with the colour of the stain and, in particular, with the stain being so small:

P1: The bloodstain ... I thought it would be bigger.

P2: And be more visible.

P3: I also thought it would be more visible.

P2: Barely saw it.

P4: But the floor felt kind of swaying when you walked on it. It felt like it was going to collapse. ...

P1: I thought it was a bit exciting that the wallpaper was torn down like this in a few places.

P2: Hard to stand and half-paint it there then.

P4: ... thought it would be more horror, scary [with the bloodstain]. I thought it would be much bigger. ...

P1: I've been there another time and then they told us that they had tried to wash [it] away and that there was blood dripping down from the ceiling, but she didn't tell us that this time.

P5: I've also heard that it dripped.

As can be seen in the excerpt, the pupils created much of the experience of the room with the bloodstain through their conversations with each other; for example, by reproducing the story about blood dripping down from the ceiling. Some pupils perceived the visit to room 13 as physical in a different way than the rest of the tour. They described the wooden floor as feeling wobbly as if it was going to 'collapse,' and that it was 'freezing cold' in the room. Thus, the experience of the bloodstain was based not only on visual impressions and the guide's commentary but also on other physical impressions and on what the pupils heard (and probably told each other) before and after the visit.

Bomtorpet: The Soldier's Cottage

Bomtorpet: The Visit

The room in the old soldier's cottage is small, and filled with various objects, paintings and photographs. The pupils, in Year 3, come from the local school and arrive at the cottage on foot. Their visit here is part of a unit of study of their local neighbourhood, which has been ongoing for several weeks. Now they will meet two representatives from the local heritage association and learn more about the local history.

The reason for the pupils' visit to the cottage is that they have been learning about the local community and its history in class (for more on this tradition, see Persson 2017; cf. Cooper 2005). Approaching history based on local history is a tradition for Swedish primary schools that can be traced back to the early

1900s and the subject of 'hembygdskunskap', that is, a Swedish version of home geography. The cottage is not the only site that the pupils will visit as part of their studies; for instance, they have also visited the local church, where they were guided by the vicar. The soldier's cottage appears in Figure 10. It is owned today by the local heritage association, and the two guides who greet the pupils, both in their 70s, have leading roles in the association. Before the visit, the pupils were asked to think of questions for the guides. The guides received the questions in advance, allowing them to plan the visit.

The room is small and cramped. After some time, and not without difficulty, everyone finds somewhere to sit. The guides sit down on two chairs at one end of the room. After the pupils have been welcomed and the guides note that 'there have probably never been so many people in this room before', they begin to address the pupils' questions, reading aloud from notes they have brought with them. The teacher sometimes intervenes and asks questions to the guides that link to things they have talked about in school. The first few questions are about the house, how old it is and who lived there. However, questions are also asked about the guides themselves, such as how old they are. The guides express their surprise at this, but reveal to the pupils that they are both in their 70s. Gradually,

Figure 10 Bomtorpet, the old cottage used to be unpainted but has taken on a modern look with painted walls and a Swedish flag. Photo: Emma Fornell, 2019. Published with permission from the photographer.

it becomes clear that a bond is being established between the pupils and the guides, where the latter are given the role of reporting from the past about a place that they all hold in common today; the local area and the present represent a reference point to gather around.

The pupils have also submitted some questions about the old grocery store, which was located on the other side of the village. This leads the female guide to point to a picture of the building where the store was once located. She talks about the store and how the local people did their shopping there, mentioning that unlike now, people used to make their purchases over the counter. She continues by connecting her childhood experience to the narrative, telling the pupils how her mother would send her to the store with a shopping list. Mainly in passing, she informs the children that she used to go to the same school as them. In this way, a bond of experience is established between the guide and the pupils. Now the conversation is changing: from having focused on the cottage and those who lived there, the pupils and guides begin to talk about what was around the cottage, about the local community they are all part of.

G2: How did Sturefors get its name? Have you been down to Sturefors, by the barn there? And the palace?

Pupils: Yes.

G2: You know it?

P1: I live there.

G2: You live there. There is a sluice and a power station. There is a small level difference in the water there, so there was a rapids there before. And then it was called Forsa. But then there was a man named Ture there, so they called it Turefors. Then around 1600 there was a lady named Margareta Sture, and she thought: could they not call this place after me? So she wanted to call it Sturefors, and eventually it went through. So that's why it's called Sturefors, from 1617 approximately.

P2: At our summer cottage our electric lawn mower is called Sture or Ture.

G1 & G2: Oh! – [laughter]

G2: Many members of the family that owns the Sturefors estate are called Ture. The lady that I was talking about, Margareta Sture, she was married to that Bielke.

Pupils: Yees.

G2: Perhaps you have not read about the Linköping Bloodbath?

Pupils: Noo.

G2: He was executed there in the Linköping Bloodbath. So she became a widow and then worked at Sturefors.

(Observation Bomtorpet)

The pictures and paintings in the room serve as inspiration for the conversation. Some pupils question the status of the images as they are not photographs and therefore do not portray the exact authentic remnants of the past.

> G2: There are a few paintings there. And a photo of the old church.
>
> G1: That picture there, it's taken there where you come over at the car park by the sports ground, where the bicycle path goes off towards the village.
>
> . . .
>
> P1: I have taken that route.
>
> G1: It is painted yes. And that one is from the other direction, it's from Norrberga farm. This is, that is now a private home, it used to be the teacher's residence a long time ago. And I think the school should be visible, I don't know.
>
> G2: That was before they built the parish home there?
>
> G1: Yes.
>
> Teacher: That's what we looked at a bit the other day, before Vist school was built.
>
> Pupils: [inaudible]
>
> [–]
>
> G2: Does anyone have any more questions?
>
> P2: In that yellow house. When we go down to the sports ground in the spring, there is usually a sea of scilla [flowers] there.
>
> G2: There usually is, it's nice.

(Observation Bomtorpet)

Here the interplay between the present and the past becomes apparent, where an experience of the present place becomes a shared reference point. In fact, this interplay touches on several different pasts, such as a relatively non-specific past regarding life at the cottage and its inhabitants; references to the Linköping Bloodbath and other events during the 1600s; and the guides' childhood memories from the mid-1900s. The conversation also becomes more open; gradually, the pupils express themselves more spontaneously. However, it is still the guides that dominate the conversation. The objects in the room, especially the pictures, serve in this way to open up the conversation, and provide a focal point around which both the guides in their 70s and the nine-year-old pupils can share their experiences.

After half an hour, the guides have answered all the pre-submitted questions, and the pupils' questions about the objects in the room ebb away. The conversation comes to a natural end, and the pupils now have the opportunity to discover the yard outside. The root cellar had previously aroused the pupils' interest, and now they are allowed to enter it and experience the cold, darkness and humidity for themselves. Otherwise, it is the privy that attracts the most attention. The pupils flock outside the open door, sharing their own experiences of using a privy. After playing a little while, it is time for snacks, and after that, the teacher gathers the class, and they head back to school on foot to continue their school day.

Bomtorpet: The Guides' Voices

Uses of the Past and the Guide's Perceived Mission

The male guide describes what he hopes to achieve and communicate to the pupils: 'That you should take care of and cherish the old, (so) that it remains . . . That you should think about it a little bit, that it should be allowed to exist for posterity, what once was . . . I hope that they take with them a little ambition to take care of things.' The female guide says she strives to narrate the 1600s in an exciting way. She describes a time travel exercise where the children participated by pushing a wheelbarrow filled with gravel and scrubbing the pine floor with soap, but that school staff dropped in bringing lunch for the pupils, and therefore 'cheated' somewhat.

Materiality of the Site

The cottage is furnished with various objects, and the female guide says that the pupils tend to ask about the rifle and if they are allowed to use it. She says that she usually replies: 'If you could shoot it, it would not be allowed to hang on the wall'. The yoke in the outhouse also raises questions among the pupils, and the guide states, 'Some are actually interested'. The privy also arouses interest, and she notes that many pupils seem to have experiences of summer houses with outhouses. She also suggests that pupils from the city probably would not have recognised a privy. She adds that pupils also ask about other objects that they find peculiar, such as the old typewriter.

The Pupils and the Site

The guide notes that this particular group of pupils was calm during the visit, which she says is not always the case. Discussing a time travel activity that had been done once before, she touches on the issue of potentially alienating the pupils from cultural heritage:

> They got names, other names . . . but today you do not know, there is not so much difference [between girls and boys] . . . And then they really got . . . The girls would do what girls did then, and the boys would not be dusting . . . I know that I asked a girl once if she had learned anything today. And she replied, "Yes, there is not only liquid soap!" . . . [The teacher] used a whole bar of soap to scrub the carpet; she had never seen that before.

She points towards a distinction between herself and the pupils when she says: 'They know so much even though they are so young! I did not know much when I was in school ... I do not think so ... For example, we did not know much about what was happening in the United States ... Now you get shown everything immediately as soon as it happens ....'

The guide presents herself as a link between the past, as it is expressed in the place, and the pupils. She creates a distance between the present and the past by suggesting that the standards of the time we live in are not self-evident and universal; for example, that women and men had other tasks a hundred years ago compared to today, and that gender equality meant something different in the past. Her view is that the pupils should get to know the place by learning about the era that Bomtorpet represents. According to the female guide, the pupils' proximity to the place and their experiences of living in the countryside provide better conditions to understand what life was like here than children from modern cities would have. The visit is rooted in a clear distinction between 'now' and 'then', according to the guide. However, the guide's empathy with the children's *erfahrung*, and her feeling of what can almost be interpreted as envy of how much pupils know today compared to what she knew at the same age, creates a bond of identification between the guide and the children.

Bomtorpet: The Pupils' Voices

Experiencing Heritage in a Local Community

Several pupils had previously seen Bomtorpet from the outside when passing by; one had bought a Christmas tree there, and one stated that she had been inside when a baptism party for her little brother was held in the cottage. Thus, it was a fairly familiar place, although for most pupils it was the first time they had been inside the cottage and the first time they had explored the yard around it. One girl said she had thought that the cottage was located further away in the woods.

At the beginning of the visit, when the class was inside the cottage, the pupils had to sit quietly while the guides answered questions and told them about the different images and objects in the room. Several pupils stated that they thought this was boring. They did not make any specific comments about the guides, although they apparently picked up some of what they had said.

The pupils had learned that many of those who had lived in the cottage had been military men. This information fitted with the name of the cottage because, as the guide told them, the name Bomtorpet could come from the fact that there was a beam (Sw. 'bom') across the road next to the cottage, or from the boom sound of a gun, but it could also be that those who lived there always missed (Sw. 'bomade') when they shot their rifles. Several pupils were also eager to explain the origin of the name of their village, Sturefors. While telling this story, they almost talked over each other. Here they helped each other to reconstruct the explanation the guides had given them.

Materiality of the Site

The main building of the cottage is a relatively small house, but several pupils pointed out that originally it had been even smaller. They spoke in great detail about how fifteen families had lived in the house and that one of them had had as many as six children, which 'is quite a lot for being a family', although one of the pupils said that her great-grandmother was the tenth sibling in her family. With six children, it must have been crowded in the cottage, the pupils thought, not least if the whole family needed to go to the toilet at the same time.

The group interviews show that the pupils had noticed several objects in the cottage, such as an iron stove, a tramp sewing machine, old-fashioned irons, paintings and rifles; some of these items can be seen in Figure 11. When the pupils referred to these objects, they demonstrated that they had seen similar objects in other places and that they had some knowledge of how they had been used. Of all the objects, it was especially the rifle that the pupils found exciting, and they explained that if the soldier ran out of gunpowder, he might have to run forward and fight with the bayonet. This was also something that the guides had told them.

Experiences of Heritage Embossed by the Pupils' Lifeworlds

The pupils became particularly excited when talking about the yard where they had the opportunity to explore. The privy, in particular, aroused enthusiasm and lively comments. This was partly about all the paper and excrement that was down in the privy hole, and partly what the privy looked like; there was, among other things, a drawing on the wall of an old man with a 'dick nose'. The pupils tried to outdo each other with stories about privies they were already familiar with from their own lifeworlds; they told a story about someone's grandmother who used to sit and read in her outhouse.

One of them speculated that if you were in the privy reading the newspaper, it could be used as toilet paper. But what would Grandpa say when he wanted to read the newspaper and found out that it had been used as toilet paper? somebody else added. In addition to the outhouse, the pupils had inspected the root cellar and an arbour. The pupils characterised the root cellar as a refrigerator of the time. They noted that there were ants in the cellar. One pupil talked about another root cellar where he had caught a spider that had crept into his nose.

When the pupils talked about the visit, there was both an explicit and an implicit comparison between now and then. They signalled that they

Figure 11 Inside the cottage. On the wall: a rifle with a bayonet. Photo: Emma
  Fornell, 2019. Published with permission from the photographer.

recognised various objects but also noted what was missing in the cottage; that
there were few books, only Bibles, and few toys. This was implicitly measured
against the yardstick of how it was in their own homes. As mentioned above,
the comparison between then and now was also present in their comments
about overcrowding.

5 Discussion

Time, Materiality and Negotiation: Experiencing Historic Sites

This project approaches critical heritage studies by investigating field trips at
the intersection of school contexts and cultural heritage practices.

The starting points for the study consist of several premises where experience and materiality are crucial for creating a multitemporal 'here and now'. We assume that the heritage connected to the sites is interpreted in a collective negotiation at the site or in the interviews afterwards. The relationship to the historic sites is a performative 'here and now'. We believe that the users of the historic site, both visiting pupils and guides, bring their experiences as resources in the negotiations. This meaning-making experience functions as collective unification during the tour and in the interviews – a 'stock of knowledge' – taken from everyday life (for the pupils) or from professional life (for the guides). The stock of knowledge comes in the form of acquaintances, such as with history learned in school or with parts of the historical canon concerning, for example, local figures or national history; and with the historic site as cultural heritage that is part of the traditional county itinerary. We further assume that the pupils' and guides' stock of knowledge is mobilised during the visit by means of the tour and the visitors' actions, physically, emotionally and verbally. Finally, we assume that haptic, visual and emotional interaction with the materiality of the historic site have a decisive impact on how the mobilisation of the stock of knowledge takes place and multitemporalities arise.

Temporal Starting Points for the Guides

The history of the place corresponds to explicit and processed knowledge on the part of the guides; that is, they have a professional and/or explicit understanding of what the place offers in terms of historical knowledge and the challenges and opportunities involved in mediating it. All guides have experiences and expectations of the visitors. How should difficult teachers be handled? How might the weather affect the visit? How does the composition of pupils affect opportunities/limitations such as whether the pupils come from the countryside or the city? How can reference points in the present be made to include all visitors; e.g., those with experiences of being newly arrived in Sweden? The 'uncertainty' that guides express is rather about reference points in the present, and how unexpected challenges may arise during the visit.

The guide at Alvastra acknowledges that history changes as new archaeological findings are made. She emphasises the role of imagination, which can be connected both to the materiality of the place (it being a ruin) and to the distance between medieval monastic life and the pupils' own experiences. The guide at Löfstad Palace considers that there is more than one way to mediate the past. She states in her interview that she strives to give the servants a role in the narrative, despite the fact that the artefacts in the palace mainly represent the history of the nobility. The leader of the role-playing game at Linköping Cathedral adapts the present to the Middle Ages. The present is a place that we leave for a historical present, a frozen time when the nuns are to be ordained, the schoolboys study scripture and the workers build the church. A clear 'now' exists and is so compelling that the activity leader remains in character even when addressing questions about the present. The guide at Motala mill site recognises that it can present problems if she chooses to wear period clothing for the tour. Inhabiting a particular historical persona can prevent her from speaking about wider processes of historical change. Finally, the guides at Bomtorpet regard the past as possessing its own agency. It is there ready to convey to visitors and the story is not adapted to different age groups or backgrounds. The past is a past that is not organised around a particular frozen moment or historical process. The artefacts of Bomtorpet are witnesses that tell of a bygone era.

The pedagogical assignment, according to the guide at Motala, is, among other things, to take the guided group's experiences as a starting point to demonstrate similarities and differences between then and now. The polarisation between a 'We' (here and now in the present) and a 'Them' (the historical figures) can however become problematic because, for example, some visitors come from poverty and overcrowded homes that are not unlike the conditions in which the workers at Motala lived. For the guide, the temporal problem in this instance is thus the present and not the past that is to be conveyed. Here a conflict arises between the guide's *erfahrung* and *erlebnis*, between the knowledge about how history should be conveyed and what is practically experienced in the meeting with visitors.

The interview with the guide at the cathedral highlights that preparations for the role play also included approaches to the religious aspects of the church. By constructing role-playing games so that the authenticity of religious practices is limited, an important historical aspect of the role play is also restricted. Medieval Sweden was Christian, but since the school is non-denominational, the time travel activity in which pupils took part should only include the social and political aspects of that period. The guide addresses the problem of including authentic religious practices in role-playing games by making a comparison with depictions of similar practices in films. When religious rituals feature in films, and are performed by actors, these rituals can be portrayed realistically but lack the religious meaning of the real thing. Similarly, the guide says, the rituals included in the role play create historical authenticity by mimicking real religious practices, without possessing real religious content and significance. However, in the pupils' conversations about religion, a temporal universal space is created when they independently (and out of nowhere) compare Christian image culture with that of Islam, where one is not allowed to make images of Muhammad.

Pupils' opportunities to physically interact with the place differ between the different sites. If Alvastra and the role-play in the cathedral are clearly physical experiences, where pupils can use their bodies when encountering the past, the visit to Löfstad Palace is of a different kind. Here, the building, its various rooms and, above all, the objects it contains are at the centre of the visit. The character of the place, that it houses artefacts that are fragile and authentically unique, sets the framework for the guide's and pupils' negotiation of the place and how it can be experienced. The guide has to tell the narrative without being able to offer the pupils direct physical contact with the artefacts. The possibilities of action, the affordances, in relation to the objects they encounter become limited. This leads to the negotiation of the place as hesitant, with little direct interaction between guide and pupils about the place, which the pupils also comment on in the group interviews. Apart from one occasion where the pupils sense a lingering scent of perfume, it is an offer of action and of meaning that points towards an experience that is characterised as *erlebnis*. An active distancing from material remnants occurs when pupils are confronted with their preconceptions about what a bloodstain should look like, and question the authenticity of the small brown stain that they find in the palace.

Just as the guide at Motala experiences a potential conflict between the 'We' in the present as a unified group with the same experiences, the guide at Löfstad Palace notes that history and artefacts need to be adapted to visitors. The chaperone chair that was used to physically separate men and women may seem unusual to visitors who come from a time where men and women are allowed to socialise freely even before marriage; however, this would not be obvious to all groups visiting Löfstad. The guide's *erfahrung* and *erlebnis* in this regard contribute to strategies for the communication of history that facilitate the bridging between then and now.

The Affirmation of Agency within the Group

The study is based on collective experiences and negotiations where guide and class together experience and interpret what they see, feel, smell and hear with support from the guide's commentary and the stock of knowledge. Part of this negotiation is made by affirming the group's agency. The guides do this explicitly in the planning of the tour by adapting and preparing for the specific characteristics of the group. An important educational task for the guide is to transform the historic site into a meaningful space and place. To be able to do so, the guides consider the age of the group and their presumed previous experiences. The guide at Löfstad Palace strives to adapt the details of the tour to whether the group consists of females or males; the curling iron in the bathroom is highlighted for a group of girls, for example. For the guides at Bomtorpet, the mission is to create respect for the past, and the community to which both the children and the guides belong is the relationship to this cultural heritage.

The guide at Alvastra emphasises her feeling of affinity with groups visiting the historic site. She says that many visitors, regardless of age, share a common reference to the traditional school trip of Östergötland, in which the monastery ruin is included. In this common reference, the starting point for both guide and group becomes a defined place and cultural heritage.

The pupils participate in the visits as part of their schoolwork and as part of the class to which they belong in school. The teachers occupy a more minor role in favour of the guide's leadership of the tour, but help the students to prepare before the visit and discuss the visit with them afterwards in class. The pupils' agency is thus under the auspices of the school and the stock of knowledge where the existing knowledge of history is used in the negotiations. This is most evident in the visits to Motala mill site and Löfstad Palace, where the classes had studied the historical period concerned.

Connections between guide and group take place in several ways. The pupils and the guides confirm each other through references to historical canon such as the Linköping Bloodbath, and figures such as Margareta Sture (Bomtorpet) and the king Gustav Vasa (Alvastra monastery ruin), to correlate the mutual stock of knowledge. At Motala mill site, the tour is guided by collective recognition. This is done through common references to the local narrative about Baltzar von Platen, the main builder of the Göta Canal who, according to the guide, most people are aware of. At Löfstad Palace, the relationship within the group is confirmed by the shared recognition of people in the portraits whom they have learned about at school.

The guide communicates with the groups by asking questions to the children, giving them tasks to solve, and answering questions from the group, which by different means create dialogues between the guide and the group. The dialogues between the pupils are further developed in the interviews, where they reason, reflect and reproduce both the visit and comments about the history that has been conveyed at the site. It can be said that their stock of knowledge has changed following the visit, since the experiences during the excursion have become a collective experience among the class. The interviews with the younger children mainly highlight the stock of knowledge from everyday life, as when the children talk about their pets. The desire to create order in experiences, a logic that the group can agree on, is shown in the example of the lay brothers (lekbröderna), where the children's everyday experience of play (leka) governs their understanding of what lay brothers were. Similarly, the division between the monastery pets' presumed homes (dogs with monks and cats with nuns) makes the content understandable to all children in the group. The pupils' immersion in a supposed world of child labour and 'brothers' who played, and their attempts to organise knowledge by giving the monks dogs and the nuns cats, show a need to organise their knowledge of the past to give meaning to history, even though the facts, in this case, were not fully correct.

The older students do not rely on their everyday life experiences in the same way. They do not negotiate the experiences of the tour in order to create a logical and comprehensible context at all costs, as with the younger ones. On the contrary, the sight of the bloodstain at Löfstad Palace provokes a critical discussion about credibility based on the limitations of the stain. Thus, materiality does not always serve to help mobilise experience so that the past emerges, but rather can stimulate, as in this case, the agency of the group in terms of critical thinking.

The experiences the pupils had in connection to the time travel activity 'Middle Ages in the Cathedral' differ from the other cases. Here, the visit was clearly framed by the role play script and the roles that pupils were given when, after counting down from now to the year 1381, they stepped into the church. In this sense, the negotiation of the place is clearly framed. However, the staging means that pupils and guides are united through roles and joint activities. Through materiality and physicality, by opening the heavy church door, singing in Latin, writing on wax tablets and smelling incense, the experience becomes physical at the same time as it becomes a collective 'We'.

Spaces with Pupils' Agency at the Centre and Spaces with Guides' and Artefacts' Agency at the Centre: Five Historic Sites

The five cases all relate to materiality and joint negotiation, yet in different ways. The historical artefacts and the materiality of each site create the conditions for different pedagogical arrangements of the visits. In the three cases discussed in Section 3, the experience of the place can be characterised as a communicative practice, where the pupils' interactions with both material remnants and the guide's frame story create the place in different ways, and where some kind of adventure is at the centre. The experience of the site is less characterised by authentic historical objects, which in this case are recreated in the guide's commentary. The ruin of Alvastra offers visual and material traces of the walls of the monastery. The material, physical milieu is also an important dimension in the monastery ruin of Alvastra. The lack of artefacts put emphasis on the place itself and the natural resources found there, such as the ruin, with its floors, masonry walls and arches, but also the plants growing on site. Not least the latter have the function of being 'time machines'. As in the cathedral role play, the guide stages pedagogical bridges between the pupils' presence at the site and the history of the place by giving the pupils tasks to solve together in pairs. By being forbidden to speak, pupils' ability to communicate physically with each other to solve problems is challenged at the same time as the knowledge of the monks' vow of silence is staged and experienced. Here, the pupils experience the site both through the help of the guide and through map-searching tasks, which make the visit to Alvastra guided by 'gamification'.

The role-playing game in the Cathedral is staged using replicas. At Motala mill site, on the other hand, artefacts and interiors are authentic and help visualise and materialise authentic scenes from the workers' everyday lives. Despite the different material conditions in the three cases, there are similarities in how the negotiations regarding the sites take place during the guided tours. The historical space is made present through empathy and experience on the part of the pupils and in symbiotic relation to the guide through the pupils' reactions and interactions during, for example, the cathedral role play. Motala mill site is presented via IRE interaction, and the objects that can be touched and which are part of the environments, such as wooden chairs, sofas, wood stove and chamber pots. Compared to the objects of noble life on display at Löfstad Palace, those at Motala and Bomtorpet are closer to the pupils' everyday lives, and thus contribute to a livelier negotiation of the place. Pupils explicitly connect the objects to their own past experiences and lifeworlds. What particularly seems to capture pupils' attention are the objects that can be related to universal needs (Radenovic & Akkad, 2022); that is, needs that can be described as transhistorical and thus linked to the foundations of human life (cf. Cultural universals, Brophy & Alleman, 2005).

The historical sites featured in Section 4 are defined by the authenticity of the artefacts in relation to the site, regardless of whether the objects may be touched or not. In both Löfstad Palace and Bomtorpet cottage, the guides' stories are shaped with support of the authentic objects. The guides invoke the cultural heritage value of the material remnants. Löfstad Palace differs from Bomtorpet by being organised as a museum with scripted tours, partly based on the life of Emilie Piper. Thus, in Löfstad the artefacts serve to illustrate an already existing narrative. The situation is different in Bomtorpet, where there is no explicitly ready-made narrative. Instead, a narrative emerges in the interaction between artefacts, pupils and guides.

Performed Temporalities A to D

Performed Temporalities A: Universality Exemplified in Materialities

Human needs for sleep, food and social togetherness are particularly high-lighted in those sites where everyday life is made visible, with both similarities and differences. At Motala mill site, the pupils observe what kitchens and cooking were like in the late 1800s through the workers' housing and artefacts. The pupils' questions about the authenticity of the artefacts – for example, whether the kitchen utensils in the exhibition were actually used by the workers who lived there – show a sense of a historical 'now' that coincides with the historical people who once, like the pupils and guides in the present, prepared food. The pupils' comments about the danger of the fire spreading from the fireplace are also an expression of their identification with the people who lived at Motala through their own understanding of the risks of fire in the present.

The everyday experience of universal needs applied to the conditions of a different time comes into play when the pupils see the mannequins crammed into the beds. Although the mannequins are obviously contemporary artefacts – one pupil tells another not to touch them – the crowding of the mannequins in the beds provokes insights into what it must have been like to live in such cramped conditions.

At Bomtorpet and Motala mill site, through chamber pots and outhouses, a temporal present is created. This is yet another example where universal needs and the intimate sphere in the form of toilet visits make it possible for pupils to make connections to past times.

Performed Temporalities B: Acquaintances Mediated in Materiality

Materiality as a common point of contact – between the pupils and the guide, but also between both pupils and guide and a historical here and now – is stimulated in the cathedral role play, where the pupils get to taste and touch herbs that were used in medicine during the Middle Ages and are still used in cooking today. During the tour of the Alvastra monastery ruin, the smell of soap from the butterbur plant stimulates the pupils' acquaintances when they learn that the monks used this plant for washing. The exposure of the plant butterbur that served as soap in the Middle Ages starts through the guide's question about the name of the plant. The pupils' experience with plants of the same material appearance is rhubarb, although this acquaintance with the sight is not correct with the actual name of the plant, the reasoning leads into the function of soap and the scent of lemon. The materiality through both the plant and the students' hands and noses, which hold and smell, creates a multitemporal meeting between students, guides and medieval monks.

Materiality, in terms of a site that becomes a common place due to shared experiences at different times, bridges guides and pupils at Bomtorpet. The guided visit to the cottage starts with a question-and-answer session where the pupils' questions are answered by the guides. Here, the temporal present is established in the discussion of the guides' and the pupils' common reference of going to the same local school. This also happens through the utilitarian items that are used to stage everyday life in the historical past. The pupils can touch and feel the artefacts, and they move through environments that clearly connect them to the past that they are experiencing in the heritage site. Their notion of this past is based on similarities and differences between now and then in regards to, for example, food. In the interviews, they note that the diet of the 1800s was meagre, while in the 1900s people were allowed to eat meat. A temporal 'now' is created when pupils ponder how cramped it must have been with several people sleeping in the same bed. Another example of this phenomenon, when pupils' experiences and interpretations of the past are based on their own lifeworlds, is when they discuss the risk of fire from the fireplace.

At Löfstad and at Bomtorpet, where materiality is defined as a cultural heritage that should not be touched but that tells its own story, the connection between *erfahrung* and *erlebnis* is not as clear and controlled as in the three previous cases, when the guides deliberately allowed the pupils' experiences to shape the tour. However, the guide at Löfstad strives to give the pupils an 'aha experience', and even argues that materiality in the form of beautiful furniture, for example, might stand in the way of the kind of historical understanding she wants to impart. It is important to her that the frozen moments represented in the various rooms and linked to the nobility – Piper's 1900s and von Fersen's 1700s – are supplemented with information about the lives of the servants. The guide also describes struggling to acquire knowledge about all of the artefacts that are housed in the museum. Thus, there is a conflict between the rich materiality and the history that the guide wants to convey. The pupils, for their part, recognise some of the people who appear in the paintings on the walls or in the guide's commentary, and connect them to what they have learned in school, thereby confirming their existing knowledge. The guide's ambition to portray the lives of the servants can be seen to succeed through the pupils' reflections on the screen in the dining room, behind which the servants would stand during meals so as not to be seen. This feeling of 'strangeness' creates a temporal and empathetic 'now'; a meeting between the pupils' experiences of how meals are conducted today and the hidden existence of the servants.

Performed Temporalities C: Imagined Materialities

A multitemporal here and now can be created through imagined materiality. A collective notion of rooms, walls, windows and doors becomes evident in Alvastra, where the guide and the pupils imagine how the monastery and the abbey church might have looked based on ruins that leave only traces of the buildings. The pupils' comments about the fun of encountering things that turn out to be something completely different from what they first thought, show that this absence of material remnants does not reduce the quality of the experience. The lives of the medieval monks, which are foreign to the pupils, nonetheless include some elements of recognition, as when the guide talks about how the monks kept warm by carrying around small dogs. Both cold and dogs are experiences that pupils and guides share with the bygone monks. However, even in environments that are rich in material remnants and provoke a high degree of recognition among the pupils, such as Löfstad Palace, an imagined materiality can take on significance, as with the supposed scent of Emilie Piper's perfume.

There are also examples of how multitemporality is created with a clear connection to the future. The imagined materiality of the mythical treasure in Alvastra leads the pupils to speculate whether the treasure will be found before they become adults. Adulthood in the future as a temporal dimension also appears when the pupils discuss the limited freedom of nuns and the prospect of not being allowed to choose who to marry.

Performed Temporalities D: Through Rituals and Materiality

Multitemporality can be created by repeating the same rituals, walking over the same floors, or touching the same objects as previous visitors. At Linköping cathedral, this idea is systematically put to use in the role play through, for example, the wax tablets and the rituals that the novices carry out. The materiality of the three knots in the rope around the novice's waist, which symbolise obedience, chastity and poverty, clearly embodies not only the nuns' dress, but central values in their monastic life. The pupils' discussion of the implications of living in a convent during the Middle Ages – both limitations, for example, in terms of freedom to marry, and opportunities for women who came from poor backgrounds – shows how their reflections on the knowledge of monastic life coexist with the experiences of living under monastic rules that are so clearly materialised in the nuns' clothes. The pupils make a temporal fusion between how they want to live their lives today (which does not correspond to the limitations that the nuns lived under) and how living conditions for some women during the Middle Ages could actually make monastic life a good alternative.

Conclusions

In both critical cultural heritage studies and research in history education, people – and the social contexts they are part of – are central when interpreting how cultural heritage is charged with meaningful content and learning. Our focus in this inductive study is on the tour and interviews with pupils and guides, is on how historic sites are created through social relations (i.e., within the class as a group), where the pupils' knowledge about the past and the materiality of the place are two important components. However, the knowledge of the past, whether it is collected at school or in the guide's material, is only one component of the process of creating multitemporalities in the historic site. The guide's pedagogical approach are the starting points for the negotiations in combination with the material conditions of the place, the artefacts, the site's links to the objects and their functional relationship to each other. The location of an iron stove in a model kitchen shows how cooking was done; crowded conditions are visualised by showing the small spaces where people lived. Artefacts alien to modern life are given meaning through their physical placement in the room next to objects that the pupils know. Knowledge by acquaintance through physical objects also serves as part of the pupils' negotiations about the historical remains. Examples of this are when the pupils interpret the kitchen stove at Alvastra as a tunnel, or the beeswax tablets as pasta during the cathedral role play. However, the spatiality of the site does not have to be materialised through historical remains to create a bond between guide and pupils, as in the Alvastra monastery ruin where the pupils and the guide 'see' the church even though only parts of the masonry materialise the site, or when pupils imagine the smell of the perfume of the deceased Emilie Piper at Löfstad Palace. Nor do artefacts have to be remnants of the past to connect the pupils' lifeworlds and experiences with the guides' stories about the history of the place, as in the cathedral role play where replicas are used as props. The physical objects and the materiality of the place become meaningful in the performative encounter. When the senses are stimulated, such as smell, hearing and touch, the multitemporal 'here and now' are created.

As we conclude the study, it is time to revisit the history education research discussed earlier. While we did not focus on pupils' learning in this study, it is clear that cultural heritage can be a valuable resource in education, as previous research has also shown (see introduction). Cultural heritage allows for knowledge by acquaintance (Winch, 2013), engaging the body and senses beyond the usual cognitive focus of history education. Our analyses of the observed tours and group interviews support this notion. We have referred to the concepts of *erlebnis* and *erfahrung* to demonstrate the different ways in which pupils can connect with the past. We have identified specific scenarios where the interactions between guide, pupils and place create opportunities for *erlebnis*. In such moments, pupils can immerse themselves in a historical present.

The five guided tours, which represent a variety of pedagogical approaches, material conditions and types of historic sites, show that pupils' and guides' *erlebnis* and *erfahrung* – that is, experience and reflection – are created in joint negotiations around materiality, where different experiences and knowledge from everyday life, history and connections to the place create a multitemporality. In this multitemporality, the recognisable, the odd, the funny and the universally natural are negotiated into something comprehensible and concrete about both the present and history.

Sources

Audio files and notes from observations, preserved at Linköping University:
Alvastra monastery ruin, 22 May 2018
Motala mill site, 30 May 2018
Linköping Cathedral, 14 March 2019
Bomtorpet, 7 May 2019
Löfstad Palace, 10 May 2019
Audio files from five interviews with guides and fourteen interviews with groups of
pupils, held in connection with the observed field trips. Audio files are preserved
at Linköping University.
Photographs of the sites, various information documents provided by the sites,
and photographs of drawings and stories that pupils produced in the classroom
after the visit. All collected materials are preserved at Linköping University.

References

Achiam, M. May, M. & Maradino, M. (2014). Affordances and Distributed Cognition in Museum Exhibitions. *Museum Management and Curatorship* 29(5), 461–481.

Arthos, J. (2000). 'To Be Alive When Something Happens': Retrieving Dilthey's Erlebnis. *Janus Head* 3(1), 77–98.

Axelsson, B. (2003). *Meningsfulla förflutenheter. Traditionalisering och teatralisering i en klosterruin*. Linköping: Linköpings universitet.

Axelsson, B. & Ludvigsson, D. (2018). Johanna, Moa and I'm Every Lesbian. Gender, Sexuality and Class in Norrköping's Industrial Landscape. In *Gender and Heritage: Performance, Place and Politics*, W. Grahn & R. Wilson (eds.), London: Routledge, 17–29.

Bakhtin, M. (1981). *The Dialogic Imagination: Four Essays*. Austin: University of Texas.

Balen, R., Blyth, E., Calabretto, H. et al. (2006). Involving Children in Health and Social Research: 'Human Becomings' or 'Active Beings'? *Childhood* 13(1), 29–48.

Bartelds, H., Saavenije, G. & van Boxtel, C. (2020). Students' and Teachers' Beliefs about Historical Empathy in Secondary History Education. *Theory and Research in Social Education* 48(4), 529–551.

Barton, K. C. & Levstik, L. (2004). *Teaching History for the Common Good*. Mahwah, NJ: Lawrence Erlbaum Associates.

Brophy, J. & Alleman, J. (2005). *Children's Thinking about Cultural Universals*. Mahwah, NJ: Lawrence Erlbaum Associates.

Carr, D. (2014). *Experience and History: Phenomenological Perspectives on the Historical World*. Oxford: Oxford University Press.

Crouch, D. (2016/2010). The Perpetual Performance and Emergence of Heritage. In *Culture, Heritage and Representation: Perspectives on Visuality and the Past*, Emma Waterson and Steve Watson (eds.), London: Routledge, 57–72.

De Nardi, S. (2020). *Visualising Place, Memory and the Imagined*. London: Routledge.

Drew, C. J., Hardman, M. L. & Hosp, J. L. (2008). Introduction to Qualitative Research and Mixed-Method Designs. In *Designing and Conducting Research in Education*, C. J. Drew, M. L. Hardman and J. L. Hosp (eds.), Thousand Oaks, CA: Sage, 183–208.

Endacott, J. L. (2010). Reconsidering Affective Engagement in Historical Empathy. *Theory and Research in Social Education* 38, 6–47.

Endacott, J. L. & Brooks, S. (2013). An Updated Theoretical and Practical Model for Promoting Historical Empathy. *Social Studies Research and Practice* 8(1), 41–58.

Erll, A. (2011). *Memory in Culture*. London: Palgrave Macmillan Memory Studies.

Gadamer, H. G. (2004). *Truth and Method*. London: Continuum.

Gibson, J. (1979). *The Ecological Approach to Visual Perception*. Boston, MA: Houghton Mifflin.

Gustafsson, L. (2002). *Den förtrollade zonen: Lekar med tid, rum och identitet under Medeltidsveckan på Gotland*. Nora: Nya Doxa.

Harrison, R. (2013). *Heritage: Critical Approaches*. Milton Park: Routledge.

Hooper-Greenhill, E. (2004). Learning from Culture: The Importance of the Museums and Galleries Education Program (Phase I) in England. *Curator: The Museum Journal* 47(4), 428–449.

Knudsen, B. T. & Stage, C. (2015). *Affective Methodologies: Developing Cultural Research Strategies for the Study of Affect*. Basingstoke: Palgrave Macmillan.

Kohlmeier, J. (2006). 'Couldn't She Just Leave?': The Relationship between Consistently Using Class Discussions and the Development of Historical Empathy in a 9th Grade World History Course. *Theory and Research in Social Education*, 34(1), 34–57.

Kvale, S. & Brinkmann, S. (2009). *Interviews: Learning the Craft of Qualitative Research Interviewing*. Los Angeles: Sage.

Larsen, J. & Widtfeldt Meged, J. (2013). Tourists Co-producing Guided Tours. *Scandinavian Journal of Hospitality and Tourism*, 13(2), 88–102.

Lee, P. (2005). Putting Principles into Practice: Understanding History. In *How Students Learn: History, Mathematics and Science in the Classroom*, M. S. Donovan and J. D. Bransford (eds.), Washington, DC: National Academies Press, 31–77.

Lonergan, L. & Andreson, L. (1988). Field-Based Education: Some Theoretical Considerations. *Higher Education Research and Development*, 7(1), 63–77.

Lovell, J. & Bull, C. (2018). *Authentic and Inauthentic Places in Tourism: From Heritage Sites to Theme Parks*. London: Routledge.

Ludvigsson, D. (2012). Student Perceptions of History Fieldwork. In *Enhancing Student Learning in History: Perspectives on University History Teaching*, D. Ludvigsson (ed.), Uppsala: Opuscula Historica Upsaliensia, (48), 63–93.

Ludvigsson, D., Johnsson Harrie, A., Stolare, M. & Trenter, C. (2020). *Vetenskaplig slutrapport: Skolbarn relaterar till historiska platser*. Stockholm: Riksantikvarieämbetet.

Ludvigsson, D., Stolare, M. & Trenter, C. (2021). Primary School Pupils Learning through Haptics at Historical Sites. *Education 3–13: International Journal of Primary, Elementary and Early Years Education* 50(5), 684–695.

Macdonald, S. (2006). Mediating Heritage: Tour Guides at the Former Nazi Party Rally Grounds, Nuremberg. *Tourist Studies* 6(2), 119–138.

Marcus, A. S., Stoddard, J. S. & Woodward, W. V. (2012). *Teaching History with Museums: Strategies for K-12 Social Studies*. New York: Routledge.

Martin, A., Ungerleider, L. G. & Haxby, J. V. (2000). Category-Specificity and the Brain. In *The New Cognitive Neurosciences*, S. Gazzaniga (eds.), Boston, MA: MIT Press, 1023–1036.

Massey, D. (2005). *For Space*. Thousand Oaks, CA: Sage.

Meurling, B. (2008). Drottningens sidentäcke: Historisk exotism och vardagsrealism i guidade visningar. *Nätverket* 15, 117–129.

Paterson, M. (2009). Haptic Geographies: Ethnography, Haptic Knowledges and Sensuous Dispositions. *Progress in Human Geography* 33(6), 766–788.

Pustz, J. (2009). *Voices from the Back Stairs: Interpreting Servants' Lives at Historic House Museums*. DeKalb, Illinois: Northern Illinois University Press.

Quinn, B. & Ryan, T. (2016). Tour Guides and the Mediation of Difficult Memories: The Case of Dublin Castle, Ireland. *Current Issues in Tourism* 19(4), 322–337.

Radenovic, L. & Akkad, I. (2022). History of Emotional Suffering: From Emotions to Needs in History of Emotions. *History & Theory* 61(1), 96–123.

Rosenzweig, R. (2000). How Americans Use and Think about the Past: Implications from a National Survey for the Teaching of History. In *Knowing, Teaching, and Learning History: National and International Perspectives*, P. N. Stearns, P. Seixas and S. Wineburg (eds.), New York: New York University Press, 262–283.

Rüsen, J. (2005). *History: Narration, Interpretation, Orientation*. New York: Berghahn Books.

Selby, M. (2016). People-Place-Past: The Visitor Experience of Cultural Heritage. In *Culture, Heritage and Representation: Perspectives on Visuality and the Past*, E. Waterson and S. Watson (eds.), London: Routledge, 39–56.

Smith, L. (2021). *Emotional Heritage: Visitor Engagement at Museums and Heritage Sites*. New York: Routledge.

Smith, L., Wetherell, M. & Campbell, G. (2018). *Emotion, Affective Practices, and the Past in the Present*. London: Routledge.

Smith, L. J. (2006). *Uses of Heritage*. London: Routledge.

Spalding, N. (2012). *Learning to Remember Slavery at the Museum: School Field-Trips, Difficult Histories and Shifting Historical Consciousness* [Diss., Newcastle University]. www.researchgate.net/publication/27257

7940_Learning_to_Remember_Slavery_School_Field_Trips_and_the_ Representation_of_Difficult_Histories_in_English_Museums.

Stolare, M., Ludvigsson, D. & Trenter, C. (2021). The Educational Power of Heritage Sites. *History Education Research Journal* 18(2), 264–279.

Sumartojo, S. & Pink, S. (2018). *Atmospheres and the Experiential World Theory and Methods*. London: Routledge.

Sylvan, T. (Ed.) (2010). *Emilies gåva: En bok om Löfstad slott*. Linköping: Östergötlands länsmuseum.

Tapper, B. (1925). Dilthey's Methodology of the Geisteswissenschaften. *The Philosophical Review* 34, 333–349.

Tiballi, A. (2015). Engaging the Past: Haptics and Object-Based Learning in Multiple Dimensions. In *Engaging the Senses: Object-Based Learning in Higher Education*, H. J. Chatterjee and L. Hannan (eds.), London: Ashgate, 75–98.

Tolly-Kelly, D. P., Waterton, E. & Watson, S. (Eds.) (2018). *Heritage, Affect and Emotion: Politics, Practices and Infrastructure*. London: Routledge.

Trenter, C., Ludvigsson, D. & Stolare, M. (2021). Collective Immersion by Affections: Children Relate to Heritage Sites. *Public History Review*, 28, 1–13.

Trofanenko, B. (2014). Affective Emotions: The Pedagogical Challenges of Knowing War. *Review of Education, Pedagogy, and Cultural Studies* 36(1), 22–39.

Wetherell, M. (2012). *Affect and Emotion: A New Social Science Understanding*. London: Sage.

Winch, C. (2013). Curriculum Design and Epistemic Ascent. *Journal of Philosophy of Education* 47(1), 128–146.

Witcomb, A. (2013). Understanding the Role of Affect in Producing a Pedagogy for History Museums. *Museum Management and Curatorship*, 28(3), 255–271.

Zerubavel, E. (2003). *Time Maps: Collective Memory and the Social Shape of the Past*. Chicago: University of Chicago Press.

Acknowledgements

Warm thanks to pupils, guides and teachers who let us follow their visits to historical sites, and for accepting to participate in interviews. Thanks to the Swedish National Heritage Board for the grant that paid for the research project [grant number 3.2.2.-5128–2016]. Thanks to Fredrik Nihlén, Linda Klementsson and Mats Sjöberg for support during the project. Thanks also to creative suggestions from Peter Aronsson, Bodil Axelsson and Cecilia Axelsson Yngveus who read an early draft of this Element.

This publication is funded by Linköping University and by the Swedish National Heritage Board R&D grant. The authors are responsible for stated opinions and factual information.

Cambridge Elements ☰

Critical Heritage Studies

Kristian Kristiansen
University of Gothenburg

Michael Rowlands
UCL

About the Series

This series focuses on the recently established field of Critical Heritage Studies. Interdisciplinary in character, it brings together contributions from experts working in a range of fields, including cultural management, anthropology, archaeology, politics, and law. The series will include volumes that demonstrate the impact of contemporary theoretical discourses on heritage found throughout the world, raising awareness of the acute relevance of critically analysing and understanding the way heritage is used today to form new futures.

Cambridge Elements ⁼

Critical Heritage Studies

Printed in the United States
by Baker & Taylor Publisher Services